Life After John 3:16

LIFE AFTER JOHN 3:16

What Your Pastor Didn't Tell You

From Salvation to Surrender

From Church Attendance to Walking in Fire

ISBN: 979-8-9942580-0-2

Published by Ordinary Man Press

Printed in the United States of America

Contact Information

For speaking engagements, bulk orders, or other inquiries, please contact:

Scott Elston

OrdinaryManPress.com

hello@ordinarymanpress.com

Dedication

To my mom, who has prayed for me more than anyone ever has or ever will.

To the men who refuse to stay silent,
The fathers who fight for their families,
and the sons who finally said yes.

To my children,
who watched me find my way back to the fire.

And to every man who's been told to wait
when God was saying go—this is for you.

And to the Holy Spirit,
who never gave up on a nine-year-old boy
standing in a rural Oklahoma church,
even when he spent forty years running.

This is Your story, told through my surrender.

Author's Note

This book reflects decades of wrestling with God, learning obedience, and discovering that His grace exceeds our delays. These stories are true parts of my journey and my family's.

The journey starts with that 9-year-old boy standing in a rural Oklahoma Baptist church. The path to writing these words has been anything but linear, marked by detours, disobedience, and divine redirection. But God has a way of making crooked paths straight (Isaiah 45:2).

Through every detour and denial, one truth remains: God's calling never left me, even when I resisted it.

My prayer is that this book meets you exactly where you are—whether you're standing at an altar for the first time, sitting in the wreckage of your own delay, or somewhere in between. It's never too late to say yes to the power God wants to release through you.

Scott Elston

Table of Contents

This Is What a Pastor Friend of Mine Had to Say

This is a fantastic read. Whether you've walked with Christ for many years or you're just beginning to explore who Jesus is, this book will meet you right where you are and encourage you to go farther.

Why? Because it unpacks for us what we need to know after we accept Jesus as our Lord and Savior. There are a lot of books that tell us when the journey begins—this one helps us understand what to do from that point on.

Scott does a beautiful job weaving his personal story together with biblical truth. He doesn't pretend to have it all figured out. He openly shares his struggles, the lessons he's learned, and the ways God has shaped him along the way. As you read, you're invited to reflect on your own story. His thoughtful questions and insights create space for deeper self-examination and growth.

I appreciate his use of humor. It adds warmth and genuineness, reminding us that the Holy Spirit often teaches us in the middle of ordinary, even imperfect, moments.

If you're looking for a book that will both ground you in truth and challenge you to grow in your faith, I highly recommend this book. It encouraged me—and I believe it will encourage you as well.

Rev. Rob Woods

Global Group Development Director for Barnabas Ministries Inc.

Chapter 1

You Made It . . . You Said Yes to Jesus

From Salvation to Surrender

You just said yes to Jesus. What happens next?

There's a gap between John 3:16 and the rest of your life. You know the verse: 'For God so loved the world . . . ' You said yes. You meant it. You felt something real. And then . . . the questions come.

I know, because I've been there.

That's just one of the questions I asked at the age of 9, standing in one of the many rows of a Baptist church in rural Oklahoma, tears streaming down my face, chest aching from whatever just happened to me.

The answer I got changed everything for me—but not in the way you'd think.

I was told, "Congratulations on finding Jesus (even though it was Jesus who found me), let's get you baptized this coming Sunday." Now, about that other thing, "Go to school. Go to college. Go to seminary. Then we'll talk." I was like, okay, it sounds good to me. What did I know? Absolutely nothing.

I thought I had time. I didn't know the attack had already begun.

This book is about what happened in those times, soon after rebirth and moving forward. That separation of time and space between the encounter of meeting the Son of God and the real world's harsh reality. Because that's where we can get lost.

That's where I got lost for so many years. And that's where the enemy does his best work, not in the dramatic moment of salvation, but in the quiet confusion that comes after.

Satan sees when and where that seed is planted and goes to work to pick it back up as quickly as he can, to steal it. If he can't get it right away, he'll try to choke it out or let the new wear off and block it from taking root. But if it gets firmly planted, that makes you a threat to a world that is opposed to God.

My Decision

I usually just sat on the pew, doodling on the back of old bulletins or on the tithe and offering envelopes during the service.

That's how it began during this three-day revival as well. But this guy, this preacher, used chalk and a black light to create these amazing pictures. Somehow, while engrossed in what he was drawing, I became engrossed in what he was saying. Then he goes and draws a lighthouse!

When the lights went out, and his black light was turned on, that lighthouse was exactly that. . . a bright light, a beacon: one that spoke to something inside of me.

What light has come into your life? Or has one not done so yet?

I don't know who was more surprised, my mother or me, as I stepped out into the aisle at the age of 9 to ask that artist-preacher how I could see the light. I remember my chest hurt, and tears were running down my face, and I had never felt anything like that before. Not only that, but I could have sworn I was called to preach, too. This is where the story begins.

That was 1974. Fifty-one years ago. And for most of those years, I thought I didn't even need to start.

Now the Questions Come

After all the tears, the initial shock and awe, the tons of questions—so the pastor is sure you understand the magnitude of this decision—you're left with one question: now what?

Here is where a 9-year-old boy stayed a 9-year-old believer. I thought I was found, but I was bound at the altar, waiting for permission to grow. That advice I was given after surrendering and being called to preach, or at the very least called to serve, left me thinking I needed a better education, a degree.

I had questions, hundreds of them over the years. Sadly, I thought the only person I could ask was the pastor in our Church. You know the same guy who said, "Come back in 15 years." Don't get me wrong, I'm not blaming my pastor, not blaming the Church. Like any kid who doesn't get his questions answered, he just moves on to the next thing. I had time on my side anyway, right?

Who Do I Talk To

Why didn't I feel like I could talk to my dad? My mom? Why not anybody else I knew who was an adult in the Church? Because, like a lot of people, not just kids but adults as well, the pastor is that go-to guy, the wise man filled with knowledge, marriage counselor, second father-like figure, and sermon giver.

Growing up, I pestered every single pastor I ever had. I had questions. I was curious. I had judgment. I looked around and saw a bunch of men telling jokes, smoking, and using curse words. I began to notice a bunch of sick people. While in church on Sundays, I saw a bunch of women and children, but few men. Who do I talk to?

There were plenty of men around—husbands, fathers, guys who led groups. I just never thought to ask them about the preaching part because they weren't preachers. But that was me being young and dumb.

Who can you talk to? You don't need someone exactly like you. You need someone who walks in faith and knows your name. Ask God to connect you—He'll either send someone to you or you to them. Be patient. They'll find you.

Let God surprise you when He answers this request.

Stories and Bible Verses

I must pause here for a moment and take into account that not everyone grew up in a church, and many still aren't. You may not know about all the Bible verses we tried to memorize and stories we listened to as children growing up in Sunday school.

Stories like David and Goliath, Joseph and the coat of many colors, Samson and Delilah, Daniel in the lion's den, Noah's Ark, Moses parting the Red Sea, and many more. They taught us all about the stories. And they are great stories. Everything from strength, faith, endurance, trust, walking in the desert with God.

But here's what they didn't teach me: what to do with the lessons I was supposed to learn from those stories. That I, too, could defeat a Goliath, I could build an ark, and I could lead others to freedom in the wake of oppression. Not just how to apply them, but to walk in that same power. They gave me history, but not discipleship—information, but not transformation.

I kept wondering what happens now, but honestly, it is WHO happens now.

Holy Spirit Come

You may not feel different yet. You may still have questions. You may still doubt. But don't mistake the silence for absence. Something—or rather *Someone*—has moved in. What comes next isn't what you do. It's who you become when you finally surrender to who He is.

"In Him, you also, after listening to the message of truth, the gospel of your salvation—having also believed, you were sealed in Him with the Holy Spirit of the promise, who is a first installment of our inheritance, in regard to the redemption of God's own possession, to the praise of His glory." Ephesians 1:13-14 (LSB)

So, to answer your question plainly: the moment you believed, you were sealed with the Holy Spirit. Not someday. Not after seminary. Right then. God doesn't wait for you to be ready. He comes when you say yes.

Maybe you're reading this because:

- ✓ You just got saved and don't know what comes next.
- ✓ You've been saved for years, but feel like something's missing.
- ✓ Church didn't prepare you for what came after the altar.
- ✓ Nobody warned you about the war that started the moment you said yes.

You're wondering: "Is this all there is?"

If any of that sounds like you, this book is your beginning roadmap to your story.

In the pages ahead, we're going to walk through some things you may have never heard after you said yes:

The attack that comes after the amen. The war nobody warned you about. The four battlegrounds where the enemy attacks: your mind, your marriage, your purpose, and your children.

Who Holy Spirit actually is—not just the Holy Ghost you heard about in church, but the Helper who lives in you right now. How to move from salvation to surrender to walking in the spirit man and not the flesh. And what discipleship looks like when it's real.

"And I will ask the Father, and he will give you another Helper, to be with you forever, even the Spirit of truth, whom the world cannot receive, because it neither sees him nor knows him. You know him, for he dwells with you and will be in you." John 14:16–17 (ESV)

And if you stick with me, we're going to discover together what happens when the Holy Spirit of God takes up residence in someone the world said didn't matter. Turns out, you're more dangerous than you think.

Chapter 2

When Believing Isn't Enough

"For God so loved the world, that he gave his only Son, that whoever believes in him should not perish but have eternal life." John 3:16 (ESV)

What We Think "Believe" Means

First, let's look at the word believe. In Greek, the word for believe, πιστεύω (*pisteuō*), doesn't mean "to mentally agree" or "acknowledge He exists." It means to entrust, to rely upon, and to cling to, to be fully committed and obedient.

It's not just faith in your mind—it's faith that moves your feet. A nod of agreement won't cut it. This kind of belief demands alignment, not just awareness. When Jesus says, 'believe in Him,' He means a life of surrender—not just an altar moment, but a life laid down. That's the invitation. That's the call.

There is a difference between simply believing Jesus lived and died for our sins and truly living in the light of and because of Him. It is the difference between knowing His name and knowing His voice.

Why We Stop at Step One

Let me ask you something:

Which comes first? The baptism or the making of disciples? Because most churches get this backwards—and that's why so many believers feel stuck.

Because wherever you were when you accepted Jesus, whether it was an altar, a living room, a jail cell, or kneeling beside your bed, that invitation to come and be "saved" from the world of woe. . . nobody said anything about becoming a disciple, did they?

And Jesus came up and spoke to them, saying, "All authority has been given to Me in heaven and on earth. Go therefore and make disciples of all the nations, baptizing them in the name of the Father and the Son and the Holy Spirit, teaching them to keep all that I commanded you; and behold, I am with you always, even to the end of the age." Matthew 28:18–20 (LSB)

If you were a child when you made that decision, *praise God for it*. If you're an adult, you might already be sizing up all the things you enjoy in life and wondering how many of them you'll have to give up. That New Year's resolution feeling is creeping in… and if you're like the rest of us, there's not a great track record after January.

But this isn't about resolutions; this is about transformation, and it doesn't come around once a year. It comes around at least once a day.

And here's the truth: I wish someone had told me on day one: you're not expected to have this figured out yet. Jesus didn't call perfect people; He called willing people.

He didn't ask for experts; He asked for followers. And every single person who's ever walked with Him started exactly where you are right now: at the beginning, unsure, a little scared, but willing to take the next step.

That's all He's asking. Just the next step. And He'll be with you for every single one.

In the beginning, salvation feels like the whole story—you got saved, you're going to Heaven, you're good. But then the Spirit starts moving inside you, and you realize there's more. A lot more. And the invitation isn't just to be rescued—it's to be transformed.

We're told, 'Say this prayer, and you'll be good.' And in that moment, it *does* feel good. Like you've been rescued and forgiven.

But no one told you that this was just the beginning of your journey. The same Jesus who saves you also asks you to follow Him. And following Him doesn't mean walking down the aisle. It means laying down your life and putting it all on the line for our heavenly Father.

So, what does that actually look like?

Following Jesus

Jesus said it plainly in Matthew 16:24, “If anyone wants to come after Me, he must deny himself, take up his cross, and follow Me.” But what people hear is:

Go to Church.
Be a nice person.
Read your Bible every day.
Pray every day.
Forgive those who've hurt you.
Don’t do any more of the ‘bad’ stuff.

That's not transformation. That's behavior modification.

The cross isn't just something Jesus died on. It's something He carried, and something you must carry too. Daily.

Some Christians don't pick it up because they were never told they'd need to. They thought *belief* was enough. But they misunderstood what "believe" really meant.

And maybe that's the scariest part? We don't really want to be free; we just want to be safe. Because freedom requires surrender. Surrender means letting go of control. For some of us, that feels like death long before it feels like resurrection.

What Comes Next

The moment you believed, you made an enemy. But Satan doesn't get the final word. The Spirit of God lives in you.

And every moment of resistance is a declaration: *not today, Satan.*

You weren't just saved to say no to sin. You were saved to walk in power. And that power comes with a name. Jesus.

So, here's the question you have to answer: Are you going to stay at step one, or are you ready for what comes after John 3:16?

Because believing isn't the finish line. It's the starting gun.

What if today is the day you stop standing at the altar and start walking with fire?

"I have been crucified with Christ. It is no longer I who live, but Christ who lives in me. And the life I now live in the flesh I live by faith in the Son of God, who loved me and gave himself for me." Galatians 2:20 (ESV)

Chapter 3

Holy Spirit: The Gift of Fire and Inheritance

If you grew up in church, you might have heard Holy Spirit mentioned in baptism formulas or benedictions. But do you actually know Him? Not just know about Him—but know Him?

When did Holy Spirit become real to you? Not just a name mentioned in church or at baptism—I'm asking about becoming a living presence in your life.

What happened the moment you asked Jesus to save you? Was there fire? Was there power? Or was there just . . . silence?

Many of us weren't anywhere special. No one told us to wait for the greatest gift known to mankind. No one even told us we could ask Holy Spirit anything—or how to do it. No one told us He's not an idea, but that He's a Person. Trinity means three, as in God, Jesus the Son of God, and Holy Spirit or Holy Ghost.

Who IS Holy Spirit?

Holy Spirit is the most misunderstood, most overlooked, and most desperately needed Person in the Trinity. We talk about God the Father. We sing about Jesus the Son. But

Holy Spirit? Only gets mentioned in passing, like a spiritual footnote.

But listen: Holy Spirit isn't optional. He isn't the "advanced level" of Christianity you get to once you've mastered the basics. He's the power source. The indwelling presence. The difference between knowing about God and experiencing God.

It's almost too simple: Holy Spirit is a Helper. A Teacher. A Wind. A Flame. The Truth. The Comforter. The very Spirit of God sent to live in and dwell inside of us.

Not visiting and not checking in occasionally. Living. Dwelling. Making His home in you.

"But when He, the Spirit of truth, comes, He will guide you into all the truth; for He will not speak on His own, but whatever He hears, He will speak; and He will disclose to you what is to come." John 16:13 (LSB)

Why Jesus Had to Leave

Jesus told His disciples that He had to go be with the Father so that Holy Spirit could come.

"But I tell you the truth: it is to your advantage that I am leaving; for if I do not leave, the Helper will not come to you; but if I go, I will send Him to you." John 16:7 (LSB)

How would you be feeling right now if Jesus, whom you now see as the Messiah, the Savior, and King, is now saying, *"It's better if I leave."*

Personally, I don't think I would have even been able to speak. I doubt if there would even be a breath left in my body to utter any sound.

These are the 'twelve' chosen by Jesus Himself! They have given up everything to follow Him. How would you feel in that moment?

But Jesus wasn't abandoning them. He was preparing them. They had walked beside Him, watched His every move, heard His every word, and broken bread with Him. But Jesus knew they couldn't do what was coming next without the Spirit that filled Him. They didn't need more sermons. They needed power. They needed a Helper.

Jesus wasn't just sending a comforter, but something bold, never seen before, a fire to live inside of us permanently! A kind of fire that would take Peter from coward to preacher. The kind that would fall on men and women in an upper room and set the world on fire with the telling of this grand love story, the gospel of Jesus Christ.

"And suddenly a noise like a violent rushing wind came from heaven, and it filled the whole house where they were sitting. And tongues that looked like fire appeared to them, distributing themselves, and a tongue rested on each one of them. And they were all filled with the Holy Spirit and began to speak with different tongues, as the Spirit was giving them the ability to speak out." Acts 2:2-4 (LSB)

And here's what we miss: that same fire is available to you. Right now. Today.

Not someday when you're spiritual enough. Not after you've read the whole Bible or gone to seminary or stopped messing up. The Spirit that fell on 120 people in an upper room is the Spirit Jesus promised to every single believer. Including you.

When the Spirit Speaks

So, what does it actually look like when Holy Spirit lives in you? How do you know? How do you hear Him?

The Bible uses two words for 'word.' Logos—the written Word, eternal and unchanging. And rhema—when God takes that Word and speaks it directly into your moment, personal and timely. That's what Holy Spirit does. He makes Scripture personal.

The Spirit that spoke through Peter that day is still speaking today. That Spirit who appeared like tongues of fire is still inside believers today. You might be driving in your car or truck, reading Scripture at the kitchen table, or hearing a song on the radio, and suddenly a verse hits you right in the middle of where you are. That's rhema. That's Holy Spirit saying, *"This one's for you.* "

He doesn't just remind you of God's truth, but helps you apply it to your soul, to your heart, to your situation, to your story.

"For to us God revealed them through the Spirit; for the Spirit searches all things, even the depths of God."
1 Corinthians 2:10 (LSB)

The fire inside us is real. So is the fight that follows after it.

And that's where most of the Church has gotten stuck. We've taught people about the Father. We've taught people about the Son. But we've been silent about the Spirit.

We've given people salvation without power. Belief without fire. A starting point without a Helper for the journey.

But you don't have to stay there. Because the same Spirit that raised Christ from the dead dwells in you. And He's not silent, distant, or waiting for you to get your act together.

God’s Spirit is already speaking. The question is: are you listening?

Chapter 4

The Attack after the Amen

The Fight You Didn't Know Was Coming — But Were Created to Win

The initial attacks often start right after accepting Jesus, in those initial moments filled with joy. These attacks usually arrive quietly, without warning or sign.

For me, it happened immediately after I invited Jesus into my life. You may wonder how an attack could reach a small 9-year-old boy in a Baptist church in rural Oklahoma.

It came in the form of tradition. It came in the missed opportunity to begin discipleship on that day. It came in the form of normalcy instead of a start to mentor and fostering a calling to preach, and instead, telling me to go to school, go to college, go to seminary, and then we'd talk.

The devil smiled.

When the battle begins, and it is real, rarely is it obvious at first glance. I smile every time I hear of people stocking up on ammunition and buying more guns. (As if they can shoot more than one at a time.) Our biggest war doesn't involve bullets; it looks more like delay and deferral, like being told, "Not yet."

The enemy rarely attacks us in the moment, but most definitely, he attacks our momentum. He'll even let you have the altar, as long as you never reach the assignment. And what better weapon than religious tradition dressed up as patience?

"Let no one look down on your youthfulness, but show yourself as a model to those who believe in word, conduct, love, faith, purity. Until I come, give attention to the public reading of Scripture, to exhortation and teaching. Do not neglect the gift within you, which was given to you through prophetic utterance with the laying on of hands by the council of elders. Take pains with these things; be absorbed in them, so that your progress will be evident to all."
1 Timothy 4:12–15 (LSB)

What Came First: Distraction or Deferment

What was your first attack after the Amen?

Was it a distraction? Did you think you had time as well? Or did you simply doubt, and hear the same voice all of us have heard at some point, that same lie, and think you don't know enough? Who or what told you to "wait" when God was saying "walk"?

What calling have you put off because someone else told you it wasn't the right time? What fire have you buried because you heard a voice inside your head that said,

"You're too young," "too broken," "too dumb and untrained"?

"But God has chosen the foolish things of the world to shame the wise, and God has chosen the weak things of the world to shame the things which are strong."
1 Corinthians 1:27-29 (LSB)

It doesn't make a difference if you were nine or ninety when God entered your life. It doesn't matter if you were raised in church and went every time the doors were open or never set foot in one in your life.

The lie we all believe is that we don't deserve it.

Well, it's not a lie—we don't.

But Jesus came and picked it all up, nailed Himself to the cross, and it all died with Him. Jesus says no one, not one person, comes to the Father except by Me.

Why?

Because it is through HIM that you were forgiven before you were born. It is through the drops of his blood upon a wooden cross and the ground where the devil thought he'd won that Jesus rose from the grave in victory over not just death, but sin, all sin—your sin and mine.

It's not about deserving; it's about being loved enough. It doesn't matter what you deserve.

Here's how it shows up:

The distraction looks like this: You get saved, you're on fire, and suddenly life gets busy. A job opportunity. A relationship. A crisis that demands your attention. None of it's evil, but all of it pulls you away from the thing God called you to in that moment.

The deferment sounds spiritual: "I need more training first." "I'm not qualified yet." "Let me get my life together, then I'll serve God." It sounds humble. It sounds wise. But it's just delay dressed up as preparation.

And both accomplish the same thing: they stop your momentum before it becomes a movement.

"But God demonstrates His own love toward us, in that while we were yet sinners, Christ died for us."
Romans 5:8 (LSB)

The Subtle War

Our war, and it is a war, isn't always loud. Most of the time, when I was growing up, it just showed up in the quiet absence of discipleship. Those subtle messages that skewed our compass by half degrees often went unnoticed. And sometimes, it's not the evil in our lives that tries to steal our calling, but good intentions that never led to obedience.

And that's why the attack feels so confusing at first: you're spiritually brand new.

Being born again is in many ways exactly like physical birth. Only now, your spirit joins in communion with God, and like any newborn, you're hungry. When you get really hungry and gain a little momentum tied in with some boldness—just like taking our first steps, letting go of the table to walk to daddy—that move draws notice in the kingdom. Our enemy takes notice.

Don't be afraid of second-guessing yourself, but don't make a decision without praying or seeking counsel from other believers. Don't let your questions cripple what God is trying to teach you, what He has placed on your heart to seek out and to learn. Doubt is brought on by fear, so fear God more than you fear the devil.

The Pushback Begins

In the beginning, salvation feels safe, like you've been, well, saved. But as transformation starts to move inside us, it can feel costly. That's where most people stop, because that's where the invitation seems to end. They believe the lie that following Jesus means giving up everything they love.

But that's also where the real battle begins.

The moment you said yes to Jesus, you became a threat. Not to God, but to the enemy. And he doesn't waste time on people who aren't dangerous to his kingdom. Satan is called the prince of this world due to the fall of man. When you receive Holy Spirit in your life, every step you take forward is in a different kingdom—the Kingdom of God.

So, the pushback starts.

Not with fire and brimstone, but with whispers:
"Did you really hear God?"
"You're not qualified for this."
"Look how you messed up. God can't use you now."
"Who do you think you are?"
"You're no better than anybody else."

The enemy's voice starts to sound like your own thoughts. He whispers just loud enough that you can't tell if it's conviction from God, condemnation from hell, or just your own insecurity.

Suddenly, you can't tell which voice is speaking anymore. When Holy Spirit speaks, the enemy is listening too. The moment light breaks in, the darkness pushes back.

Every word you speak into existence, just like in a court of law, can and will be used against you. So, when you pray, pray out loud so the devil knows you're no longer his. Tell the world who you are, shout it out, "I'm a child of God, an heir to the kingdom of God! I was chosen, and I am loved!"

And here's the truth: most people don't realize this isn't happening because you díd something wrong. It's happening because you did something right. You chose to follow Jesus.

Because when you rise in your own home, hell loses ground it never expected to give up. If you're getting hit, it's because you're finally standing up.

"For the weapons of our warfare are not of the flesh, but divinely powerful for the destruction of fortresses. We are destroying arguments and all arrogance raised against the knowledge of God, and we are taking every thought captive to the obedience of Christ." 2 Corinthians 10:4-5 (LSB)

Chapter 5

When Good Intentions Become Weapons

Those First Moments after Salvation

In Chapter 4, I told you about the first attack after I said yes to Jesus—how tradition and well-meaning advice told a 9-year-old to wait 15 years before starting what God called him to do that day.

But here's what I didn't tell you: those people loved me. They weren't trying to hurt me. They thought they were protecting me and guiding me, helping me.

And that's exactly what makes this attack so *dangerous*.

We do this to our own kids, too, don't we? When they ask spiritual questions, we say, 'You're not ready yet.' Or 'Let's talk about it later.' I've done it and made my own children wait for answers God wanted to give them right then.

But then I caught myself. I remembered what it felt like to be told to wait when God was saying 'go.' And I realized: the attack that delayed my calling was the same one I was using on my kids.

Anyone can be used against us. It's not always out of hate or pride or spite. Sometimes it's out of love. A love filled with good intentions. A wrong word. A well-meaning opinion. A fear-driven decision. Families split, hearts break, and silence sets in. And a lot of the time, it's over things that aren't even close to being as thick as the blood that ties us together. Lately, it's been about religion. About who raised whom the right way or not. Or what example we did or didn't set as parents, husbands, daughters, or friends.

This battlefield called Earth is mostly subtle. Quiet. Most of the time when I was growing up, it didn't come with flames or fists. It came in the form of absence. The quiet absence of discipleship. The slow fade of spiritual attention.

The tiny battles showed up in small, barely noticeable ways. Little off-ramps from the road God put you on. . . And it's not always the evil in our lives that steals our calling. Sometimes it's good intentions that never lead to obedience.

How This Looks in Real Life

Let me show you three scenarios. I guarantee you've either experienced one of these or witnessed it. And in every case, nobody meant harm. That's what makes it so hard to spot.

Protective Parent

A teenage girl says she feels like God wants her to go on a mission trip. She's lit up about it. Her eyes are shining, her Bible's open, and she's asking real questions. But her parents—good, loving, Jesus-following parents—say, "Sweetheart, the world is dangerous. You can serve God here." They mean well. They're afraid. And fear talks louder than faith sometimes. So, they shut the door and call it wisdom. But what they really did was cover obedience with bubble wrap.

Wait Your Turn

A man feels the Spirit nudge him to start a small prayer group at work. Nothing fancy. Just coffee, Scripture, and some honest prayer in the break room.

He tells his pastor first, just wanting to make sure he's not out of line. And the pastor says, "Let's wait and see. Timing matters." The man listens. Years pass. He never does it. Not because he didn't want to, but because he waited for permission when God had already given it.

The pastor wasn't cruel. He was cautious. But the caution killed what God was trying to birth.

Church Committee

A woman wants to start something simple: bring meals and prayer to single moms in her town. She volunteers. She shares the idea. The church says yes.

After she fills out the forms, finishes a class, and gets the board's sign-off, she waits. She follows the steps. Weeks turn to months. The fire dims.

Her yes gets buried under the paperwork. The people meant to protect the Body ended up muzzling the Spirit. Not because they were evil, but because they trusted the process more than the prompting.

Finding Your People

These stories aren't rare. They happen in churches, families, and small groups every single day. Good people with God-given ideas are being told to sit down, slow down, fill out forms, or just wait.

So, what do you do when the people you trust, the ones who were supposed to guide you, end up becoming the very ones who hold you back?

Not out of hate, not even out of sin, but out of fear or tradition or plain old hesitation?

You can't cut everyone off. And you don't give up on the Body. You go looking for the ones who listen when God speaks. The ones who won't clip your wings just because they've never flown. The ones who tell you, "If God said it, go."

Separating yourself from temptation and sin isn't about hiding from the world. It's about *finding your people—the* kind who won't let you quit. The ones who sharpen you, fight for you, and pray when you're too tired to speak. The ones who don't just talk about faith but live it in the middle of the mess.

That's when the Body of Christ stops being a sermon and starts becoming a shelter.

But finding your people also means knowing how to spot the ones who aren't. And that's hard, especially when the voice speaking doubt comes from someone you love.

Sometimes it's your dad. Your pastor, or maybe even your spouse.

Someone who changed your diapers or held your hand through the worst. So how do you know if they're holding you back because they see something you don't—or because they're afraid to let you grow?

Here's one way to tell:

Fear always focuses on *what might go wrong.*
Faith asks, "*What if God shows up?*"

Fear points to your weakness.
Faith points to His strength.

Fear says, "Be careful."
Faith says, "Be obedient."

That doesn't mean you ignore wise counsel. But it does mean you line it up with Scripture—every time. And you ask the Spirit to confirm what's true and strip away the rest.

And what if it's your own family? What if the resistance comes from inside the house?

That's the hardest kind. Because it doesn't come wearing the face of the enemy. It comes with the smell of your mama's cooking. It comes in the voice that tucked you in at night or taught you how to pray. And still, if obedience to God costs you comfort in your own home, then you follow anyway. Jesus said it would happen. He wasn't vague about it.

“A person’s enemies will be the members of his household. The one who loves father or mother more than Me is not worthy of Me . . . and the one who has found his life will lose it, and the one who has lost his life on My account will find it.” Matthew 10:36–39 (LSB)

That’s not easy. But you don’t walk it alone. Even Jesus walked with twelve. And He knew one would betray Him, another would deny Him, and the rest would scatter. Still, He chose community. And He called them friends.

"Do not be deceived: 'Bad company corrupts good morals.' Sober up morally and stop sinning, for some have no knowledge of God. I say this to your shame."
1 Corinthians 15:33–34 (LSB)

You weren't meant to walk this alone. But you also weren't meant to let good intentions become chains.

"Two are better than one, because they have a good return for their labor; for if either of them falls, the one will lift up his companion. But woe to the one who falls when there is not another to lift him up!" Ecclesiastes 4:9–10 (LSB)

Find your people. The ones who hear God and aren't afraid when you do too. The ones who say 'go' when the Spirit says 'go.' The ones who would rather see you obey God and fail than disobey Him and succeed.

Because the fight you're in isn't against the people who love you. It's against the fear, tradition, and control that keeps all of us from becoming who God called us to be.

And sometimes the most loving thing you can do, for yourself and for them, is to say yes to God anyway.

Chapter 6

The War Nobody Warned You About

The Reality We Didn't Learn

This concept of struggling against rulers and authorities, world forces of darkness, spiritual forces of wickedness in the *"heavenly"* places? Really? Me?

"For our struggle is not against flesh and blood, but against the rulers, against the authorities, against the world forces of this darkness, against the spiritual forces of wickedness in the heavenly places." Ephesians 6:12 (LSB)

How on earth do we contend with something like this? The better question is, why have we been so afraid of teaching our children how to defend against this?

If we aren't being taught about who Holy Spirit is, why would we teach about who the devil is? Could it be fear?

When the world around us began to decay, when participation regardless of effort was rewarded, and God and prayer were removed from schools, we brought into existence a spiritual generation raised on behavior management, and not spiritual authority.

We raised and taught our kids how to "be good" but not how to stand up, to stand firm.

We weren't trained, not because people didn't care, but because they were too afraid to go there. Afraid to name the enemy, any enemy. Afraid or unsure of how to call on the Helper. Thinking that if we didn't mention his name, he would leave us alone.

Well, he did leave us alone and instead focused on our children, our future educators, our future parents. Our identity. The prince of the air (waves) became the babysitter for Western culture.

What we feared most of all wasn't God or Satan. It was a loss of control, yes, control.
Because when you start talking about spiritual warfare…

You also have to talk about power (God's power), authority (Kingdom Authority), and our desperate need for dependence on Holy Spirit.

And that takes the spotlight off humanity and puts it back where it belongs, on God's Spirit moving through weak people.

Like Adam and Eve, we began to diminish and lose that spiritual inheritance because the truth was withheld.

"My people are destroyed for lack of knowledge. Because you have rejected knowledge, I also will reject you from ministering as priest to Me. Since you have forgotten the law of your God, I Myself also will forget your children." Hosea 4:6 (LSB)

The silence wasn't neutral. When we stopped teaching about the enemy, we didn't make him go away; we just stopped recognizing him.

When we stopped equipping our children with spiritual authority, they grew up defenseless. And now we wonder why a generation raised in church walks away the moment life gets hard.

They were taught to be nice, not to be mighty. They were given rules to follow, not power to stand. And the enemy? He's been training his army for centuries, while we've been managing behaviors in place of mentorship.

How the Enemy Actually Works

We've got more knowledge of urban legends than we do of what it means to fear the Lord.

We fear superstition more than the cost of our silence. We keep telling ourselves it's none of our business, while the enemy keeps making it his.

Have we taught ourselves to fear more of superstition than sin? Traded reverence for ritual and tradition? Boldness for silence? We fear bad luck more than we fear disobedience.

And the enemy? He's doing his best work by keeping you distracted, numbed out, and passive.

But let's be clear about how he actually operates. The enemy doesn't always show up with obvious temptation.

Most of the time, the enemy uses three simple weapons:

Accusation: *"You're not good enough. Look at what you did. God can't use someone like you. You failed too many times. You're too broken."*

Isolation: *Making you think you're the only one struggling. Convincing you that if anyone knew the real you, they'd walk away. So, you hide. You perform. You pretend.*

Distortion: *Taking something true and twisting it just enough, using Scripture out of context, and making God's voice sound harsh and condemning instead of correcting and loving.*

He doesn't need you to become evil. He just needs you to stay comfortable. He doesn't need you to curse God; he just needs you to stay quiet.

And remember this: When Holy Spirit speaks, the enemy is watching and listening to prepare some interference or distraction. The moment light breaks in, the darkness pushes back.

Look at how Satan uses pride. We walk past a homeless person. We see someone struggling and judge them instead of helping them. Remember the story Jesus told?

"And by chance a priest was going down on that road, and when he saw him, he passed by on the other side. Likewise, a Levite also, when he came to the place and saw him, passed by on the other side." Luke 10:31–32 (LSB)

Religious people. Good people. They saw the need and walked right past it. Why? Because they had somewhere to be. Because helping would be messy. Because they convinced themselves it wasn't their responsibility.
The enemy has done his job well in creating in us a sense of pride and accomplishment that makes us better than everyone else. Better than the broken. Better than the lost. Better than the ones who "should have known better."
But Jesus didn't die for the ones who had it all together. He died for the ones bleeding on the side of the road.

Where the Battle Really Is

We walk past broken people. We scroll past spiritual wreckage like it's just background noise.

We saw that homeless guy and thought, "He probably did it to himself."

The war is raging right here… in our own heads, our homes, our marriages, and in the hearts of our children.

This isn't speculation. The world and our enemy have made it personal.

The battleground isn't some distant place where super-Christians fight demons in dark corners. The battleground is you.

We hear the Spirit nudge us to speak up, and we say, "That's not my place." That's where the enemy sets up camp. That's where the lies start sounding like your own thoughts.

Yeah, the enemy has been doing this for a very long time. Not with horns and pitchforks, but with pride. With comfort. With our own sense of being "good enough."

And here's the truth most of us never knew or got warned about:

This war? It doesn't start in the White House or the courthouse.

It starts in your house.

So, let's go there.

The next four chapters are going to take you through the four primary battlegrounds where this war is being fought right now, today, in your life:

Your Mind – *Where the lies sound like your own voice and the battle for truth is fought in your thoughts.*

Your Marriage – *Where covenant is under attack, and the enemy works to divide what God joined together.*

Your Purpose – *Where delay, distraction, and discouragement try to bury the calling God placed on your life.*

Your Children – *Where the enemy targets the next generation before they even know they're in a fight.*

This isn't theory. This is the ground you're standing on right now.

Chapter 7

The Battleground: Your Mind

"Be sober-minded; be watchful. Your adversary the devil prowls around like a roaring lion, seeking someone to devour." 1 Peter 5:8 (ESV)

The Battle Starts in Your Head

Being sober-minded means being humble, focused, and in control of our emotions and our thoughts. Our thoughts are formed from our experiences, our interactions with others, and overhearing or being involved in conversations. Especially those topics that trigger a reaction, anger, or joy. Are we fighting mad or joyfully made today? Let's see how well you do in traffic.

I remember going to church for Saturday morning men's coffee one day, and I was not a happy camper. I don't know what I was mad about. Seems like I was angry all the time back then. A friend of mine looked at me and stated rather matter-of-factly, "You know you choose to be mad." I said, "What? I didn't choose anything; they were the ones . . .." I have no idea now. It's hard to admit the truth or that someone else is right when you've spent your whole life thinking you are the one who is always right. Hence, the numerous days of anger.

"Be angry and do not sin; do not let the sun go down on your anger, and give no opportunity to the devil." Ephesians 4:26–27 (ESV)

I didn't know it at the time, but my unaddressed anger, my quiet disagreement with life, was more than just a feeling. It was an unlocked gate. A place where I'd fallen asleep on watch.

Not a gaping hole the enemy could charge through. Nothing that obvious. Just a moment where I wasn't watching. And that's all he needs. One unguarded moment at a time. One compromise. One ignored warning. And before you know it, he's over the wall.

Most of us never look up. We just assume the wall's holding because nothing's fallen on our heads yet. Or we think we're fine because we haven't been called out where we're lacking.

Just because things are going well doesn't mean we're living right or that we have God's favor. Sometimes we're just coasting on His grace while the cracks get deeper.

We assume silence from heaven means approval. It doesn't. Sometimes it just means God's giving us time to come clean. Time to wrestle with the truth in our minds.

The wall God's asked us to build isn't made of image or pride. It's not about keeping people out or covering up what's going on inside. It's not just a wall of defense. It's a wall of *watching.* A wall where you stand guard for the kingdom. Being constantly at a state of readiness.

"I searched for a man among them who would build up a wall and stand in the breach before Me for the land, so that

I would not destroy it; but I found no one."
Ezekiel 22:30 (LSB)

God's not asking for perfection. He's asking for presence. God is seeking someone awake who sees the cracks and doesn't wait for someone else to fix it.

Every compromised thought is a brick out of place. Every lie we tolerate. Every emotion we stuff down and never name. These things don't seem like much, but they do add up. And over time, the enemy can find his way in.

Here are the questions we should ask:

Where's the breach?

Am I standing in it, or just hoping someone else will?

Your Mind is a Liar

Your mind tells you a great many things. It's the receiver of information from the soul: the conduit where Spirit and flesh speak into your life. It is the biggest liar you will ever know. It's also the control center, where thoughts are captured, emotions chosen, joy embraced… or the world is allowed to destroy your peace of heart and mind.

Your mind ever told you something that felt true… but wasn't? Mine has. More times than I can count.

That's the thing. Your mind isn't neutral. It doesn't just receive information and hold it for safekeeping. It sorts it. It speaks it back to you. Twists it around. Sometimes it repeats the truth. Sometimes it repeats the trauma. Sometimes it just flat-out lies.

It's never obvious. It's usually subtle. Familiar. And that's why it works.

"You're not ready."
"You're too broken."
"God couldn't use you."
"You're the problem."
"You've missed it."
"You're alone."
"You'll never be free."
Sound familiar?

Most of those lies don't start as lies. They come as simple thoughts. They sound like our own voice. They use our memories, our disappointments, and our timelines.

But if we don't catch them, they take root. They stop being passing thoughts and start becoming strongholds. Beliefs. Mindsets. They become 'our truth'.

That's how deception works …nobody believes they're deceived or knows they're caught in one.

That's how strongholds work. One brick at a time. Until the lie feels like your identity or your destiny.

You stop seeing yourself through the Word and start seeing yourself through the eyes of the world. A world filled with fear of being second best. Some old label someone gave you when you were thirteen still echoes from the shadows. That's the lie.

The enemy doesn't need you to rebel. He just needs you to agree with something God never said.

That's how the war starts. And the battleground? It's not out there somewhere. It's right here in your mind.

How many times have we trusted our own thoughts more than we've trusted the voice of God, been impatient for an answer to prayer, acted without clarity, and it has cost us?

"We are destroying arguments and all arrogance raised against the knowledge of God, and we are taking every thought captive to the obedience of Christ."
2 Corinthians 10:5 (LSB)

That's not passive language, the Apostle Paul is saying here. That's telling us it's a fight.

You cannot counsel a lie. You don't pet it or negotiate with it. You take it captive. You bring it to Jesus and ask, "Is this true?"

If it's not, it doesn't get to stay. But here's the part we don't talk about enough: you can love God and still be believing lies. You can serve, tithe, go to church, and still have strongholds in your mind that are keeping you stuck.

That doesn't mean you're a failure. It means you're in a fight. It means the devil knows you're important, and he's not going to stop coming at you.

And the first step to freedom is recognizing you're not crazy. You're in a battle. So, when the lies come—and they will—don't just let them sit.

When the thought comes: *"I'll never be free."*
Answer it: *"Whom the Son sets free is free indeed." (John 8:36)*

When the thought comes: *"I'm too broken."*
Answer it: *"His power is made perfect in weakness." (2 Corinthians 12:9)*

You don't win the fight by being loud. You win by knowing what's true.
You win by saying, *"I'm not going to let my thoughts run my life anymore."*

You win by surrendering the war in your head to the One who already won the battle against sin and death.

So let me ask you the question I had to ask myself:

What lies have I agreed with that God never said?

Because whatever that is. . . **it's time to tear it down.**

Taking Thoughts Captive

Which Voice Wins?

Right here, in this moment, is where so many fall back. The pull of the past feels familiar. The voice of fear starts whispering. The old crowd shows up just when you're trying to walk away. But this is the crossroads. The sacred point of separation.

Don't mistake this for a season of isolation. It's not about being alone. But it *is* about being set apart from the stumbling blocks, the old cycles, the voices that want to pull you off the path before your feet even get steady.

My son was angry at me once for telling him to do something he didn't want to do. It wasn't anything huge, just something that required getting up and off the couch. I saw the look on his face, so I asked him a question that caught him off guard: "Who are you listening to right now?"

He looked confused. So, I tried to explain. I told him I picture it like this, every one of us has a little angel on one shoulder and a little devil on the other. *I know that's not theology, but it paints the picture.* They both whisper. And we choose which one of them is going to win.

Even in little moments, cleaning your room, taking out the trash, doing what you don't feel like doing, the war is on. We think the battle is in our minds. But the mind is just where it lands. The real war? It's in the soul.

I know that's oversimplified, the whole angel and devil on your shoulder thing, but it helped him see the truth: every moment, we're choosing which voice wins.

And every time we choose to obey, even in the small stuff, we're telling the enemy, *I turn my back on you.*

We don't always realize it, but the devil pays attention to how we respond to the smallest things, not because the trash matters, but because our obedience does.

Here's the truth: you always have a choice. You don't have to let that voice of reason and justification win. You can choose the voice you hear in your Spirit.

As a teenager, I had this habit. I don't even remember where I picked it up. But when I was wrestling with a decision or situation, a temptation, anger, or fear, I would literally turn to my right and take two steps. It was my physical way of turning toward Jesus.

Then I would say out loud, "Get behind me, Satan. I want Jesus." That may sound silly to some. But it worked. There was peace. Clarity. The distractions got quiet. Not because I was strong—but because I chose who I was listening to.

I remember when my daughter was sick. Those thoughts of what I would do if she died. How would her younger brother react? I drove back and forth to California every week, so I was a captive audience. But I still applied my rule. I simply turned my head and told Satan to get out of my truck. Every time, I felt God's peace replace that fear.

"Be of sober spirit, be on the alert. Your adversary, the devil, prowls around like a roaring lion, seeking someone to devour. So, resist him, firm in your faith, knowing that the same experiences of suffering are being accomplished by your brothers and sisters who are in the world."
1 Peter 5:8–9 (NASB 1995)

The enemy doesn’t give up easily. But neither does the Spirit of God.

Every moment you resist is a declaration: *not today, Satan.* But it’s more than resistance. Resistance is part of the battle. But it’s not the whole thing. You weren't just saved to say no to sin. You were saved to walk in power, to obey when it costs you, to carry purpose—not just survive the day.

So, how do you actually take a thought captive?

It starts like this:

Recognize the lie. That thought, *“I’ll never change,”* doesn’t sound evil. But is it true?

Call it out. You may need to say it out loud: *“That’s not what God said about me.”*

Replace it with truth. Find Scripture. Say it. Write it down. Fight with it. Pray over it.

Lie: “You’ll never change.”
Truth: “If anyone is in Christ, he is a new creation. The old has passed away.” 2 Corinthians 5:17

Lie: “God’s done with you.”
Truth: “I am convinced that neither death nor life…can separate us from the love of God” Romans 8:38-39

Lie: “You’ve messed up too much to be used.”

Truth: “My grace is sufficient for you, for My power is made perfect in weakness.” 2 Corinthians 12:9

Taking a thought captive isn’t just about stopping the lie. It’s about choosing the truth. And that truth has a name. Jesus.

You don’t have to live by the voice that’s always shamed you. Always reminding you of your past. You don’t have to follow the thought that says you’ll never get free. And my favorite, "I know what you did."

God knows what you did, so He sent His son to take it from you. The power that raised Christ from the dead lives in you. That means the war in your head isn’t where it ends.

Take charge and take captive those lies and past reminders and throw them away with the trash.

What if today’s the day you stop standing at the altar begging for a forgiveness that's already been given… and start walking with fire?

What thought have you let run loose in your head for way too long?

Chapter 8

The Battleground: Your Marriage

Covenant vs. Commitment

You're not just fighting for your comfort, you're fighting for your covenant.

I wish I could say I am an expert in this area, but I'm not. I got married out of loneliness while in the military to a girl from back home. I was grounded, and she was like living with lightning. As I look back now, the teenage drama, jealousy, doubt, mistrust, and fear couldn't have been any worse. I actually asked God for permission to marry her. His answer was yes.

The yes answer came with a warning. I had just found that church a few months earlier, where I finally met Holy Spirit. I was on top of the world, but lonely. I was told that if "I" did not stay in a relationship with the church, the body, and with God, I would lose my family. I didn't know what that meant, but I knew I could do it. I was committed. But I didn't know what that meant. I was under a covenant, and I had never heard of it.

My daughter was one when she left. I had failed to stay in any body of believers, strayed from being the spiritual head of the home. I didn't reserve any time to pray or read or even think of God in those days. My excuse was that being stationed in Germany, there were few places to worship. The real reason is I got wrapped up in life, in fear.

After returning to the States and attempting to find a church, I kept getting met with excuses. The day I put my foot down and informed her I was going to church with or without her, and I did, she left. She didn't believe in God the way I did, she told me later. Years later, I prayed for three days, begging for a way to get my family back. I loved my in-laws like they were my own parents. That answer was no. "It is too late; she is not receptive to me."

I didn't understand my commitment to the marriage and my covenant with God for the marriage.

"If the foundations are destroyed, what can the righteous do?" Psalm 11:3

That loss taught me something I wish I'd known earlier: there's a difference between commitment and covenant. Commitment says, 'I'll try.' Covenant says, 'I'm bound.' Commitment is personal. Covenant is before God.

And somewhere along the way, our culture lost the difference.

Marriage statistics have plummeted since the 1970s, right around when the 'If it feels good, do it' movement took a foothold. Funny, I can't find that in scripture anywhere.

Those sacred things and sanctity of marriage, which they wouldn't even show on television, slowly began to disappear. Conflict entertainment was born, humor that used race and bias became the norm, and it became profitable. The enemy has watched human nature for thousands of years, but we forgot about him. The prince of the power of the air.

"And you were dead in your transgressions and sins, in which you formerly walked according to the course of this world, according to the ruler of the power of the air, the spirit that is now working in the sons of disobedience." Ephesians 2:1–2 (LSB)

We exchanged the word covenant for the pursuit of happiness, reducing marriage from a sacred promise to personal preference. Or did you choose those emotions too? Life stopped being about what we needed and became about what we wanted. Our identities began to morph into free-flowing whims and desires without boundaries, instead of being anchored in who God created us to be.

We stopped being set apart. The world didn't hate us anymore. We'd become one with Mother Earth. We no longer needed necessities; we needed niceties. Bigger, better, with enough room to entertain and hope everyone will love us or leave us alone.

Covenant became an old man's word; we needed something new, something stylish, something convenient. We traded sacred for stylish. But the trade cost us more than we knew.

The age of I need it now, quick, fast, and in a hurry, replaced patience with wantonness. We broke from faithfulness to feelings, from being image-bearers of God to image-managers of ourselves. That trend began long before social media. Now it's nearly perfected. It was all planned.

How the Enemy Attacks Marriage

Most people think the enemy only shows up in a marriage when someone cheats, or when there are constant fights and yelling, slammed doors, or separate bedrooms. But that's not always how it starts. The enemy is patient. Subtle. Strategic.

He doesn't need to blow your house down if he can get you to leave the door unlocked. Sometimes the attack comes in the form of silence. It comes in the form of family and career busyness. Or both of you scrolling on your phone or watching television in bed until one of you rolls over and turns out the light.

Sometimes the attack is exhaustion. Sometimes it's spiritual numbness, when you're too tired to fight, so you don't. Remember, if Satan can't kill your marriage, destroy it, or steal it, he will make it ineffective through numbness or exhaustion.

There was a time when my second daughter was born, we thought me working nights was cheaper than daycare. When exhaustion came, so did frustration. The separation began before we knew what was happening. We tried, but communication was at a minimum. Even changing jobs and having another child wouldn't save it.

By the time we both realized we should probably go back to church, the damage was done. Without prayer and forgiveness, resentment sets in. That attack comes daily, reminding you of what each other had or had not done.

The truth is, not praying together is one of the first signs the battle has begun. But it's almost never seen that way. It just feels like survival. Like one more thing on a long list. You say, "We'll do it tomorrow," until you forget what praying together even feels like.

You don't drift toward covenant. You drift away from it.

"Be alert and of sober mind. Your enemy the devil prowls around like a roaring lion looking for someone to devour." 1 Peter 5:8 (NIV)

Distraction is one of his favorite weapons. Not all distractions are an attack, but they can certainly end up becoming one. Many think of more important reasons, like pornography or infidelity. In reality, all it takes is just good old-fashioned distraction.

It starts with those little fires you have to put out. Deadlines. Bills. Appointments. Sports. Work. Everything that feels urgent but isn't eternal.

Eventually, you become partners in parenting or projects, but not in presence.

You stop looking at each other in the eye. You stop checking in on the soul.

You talk about plans, not love. You begin to look past one another. And before long, the covenant feels cold.

While serving with the Sheriff's department, which I absolutely loved, I would take extra shifts or cover for someone. That brotherhood feeling and camaraderie were more fun than my marriage. The conversations were light-hearted without the worry of stepping on toes.

The enemy doesn't always bring chaos. Sometimes he brings comfort that leads to coasting. Sometimes he brings fatigue that sounds like "not now."

Sometimes he brings silence that feels like peace, but it's really the absence of connection.

He doesn't need to destroy your marriage. He just needs to convince you that it's not worth fighting for. And the longer we let that voice linger, the easier it is to believe. We start thinking distance is normal. That roommate is just a part of "growing older." That covenant was for another season of life. But not now.

That's a lie. Because a covenant doesn't age out, it deepens if you let it.

You don't stay married just because you said, "I do." You stay married because you keep saying "yes" to the fight. Yes, to what's sacred.

Yes, to what belongs to God, not just to you.

If you chose to stay, if you had to ask God to help you love your spouse again, you honored that covenant by staying in the fight. It was never about someone else or wasting money, or lack of communication, but about trust and respect, not just for your husband or your wife, but for yourself.

I'm just as guilty as the next person who gets upset if I don't get the response I expected. If I didn’t see the results I was hoping for. When the agreement we had made was broken, my wife did the exact opposite of what we had agreed upon—or what I thought we'd agreed upon. How much do we all assume that we are understood when we speak? How many bricks have mortar missing around them due to assumptions?

Where have you assumed instead of asking? What’s one place in your marriage that needs repair, not just reaction?

“Let us not lose heart in doing good, for in due time we will reap, if we do not grow weary.” Galatians 6:9 (LSB)

It's not if we’re perfect. It's if we don’t quit!

Fighting For What's Sacred

You can’t protect what you won’t fight for. And you won’t fight for what you no longer see as sacred. Marriage isn’t a contract you renew when it's convenient. It’s a covenant you guard when it’s under fire.

So, what does that look like?

Sometimes it means praying when you don't feel connected. To God or your spouse. Sometimes it's listening when you'd rather be right. Sometimes it's asking God to help you love again because your feelings dried up a long time ago. Asking God to help you trust or forgive again, one more time.

Sometimes fighting for your marriage doesn't feel like a war.
Sometimes it just feels like keeping your mouth shut.

I remember a conversation about having "meaningful communication." Just talking about work wasn't enough. She needed more. And I agreed. I said tomorrow would be the day. I'd go home and be a better listener, a better communicator.

I walked into the kitchen and declared, "I'm ready!" I listened for thirty minutes about how her day went. No interruptions. No comments. No attempts to fix anything. I just listened. She smiled and kept fixing dinner. I kept my mouth shut.

That may not sound like much. But in that moment, that *was* the fight.
Not to win. Not to be heard. Just to be present.

Fighting for your marriage doesn't always look spiritual. Sometimes it looks like taking your spouse on a date when money is tight. Making coffee before they wake up.

Turning off the phone and sitting down on the couch when there are a hundred other things to do.

It's saying, "How can I serve you right now?" instead of "What about me?"

I've got a really bad habit of waiting until my wife gets up to get a drink or refill, and hand her my glass or ask for something else. While it has become a running joke, it still is selfish. I think we both see how long we can hold out to see who is going to get up first. One day, we might die of thirst. But seriously, that's what happens when we stop serving each other. We both end up empty, waiting for the other person to move first.

It sounds funny, and it is, but it also says something deeper. We get so used to being served, we forget to serve. We start measuring who does what, who got up last time, and who carried the weight this week.

And that's when love turns into keeping score.

This fight isn't just to stay together. It's to stay *one.* And the only way that happens is if Christ remains in the middle. Start praying together, even if it's awkward, even if it's short. Start small. God honors the obedience, not the polish.

Talk about Scripture. Ask each other, "What's God been showing you?" Make spiritual conversation normal again, not just when you're in crisis. Stop assuming you know what the other person is thinking or feeling. Ask.

And then actually listen.

This is what it means to guard what's sacred. Not with control. But with commitment. With surrender. With the kind of love that doesn't walk away just because it got hard.

It's not your job to bring about change in your spouse. You can't. It *is* your job to pray. To ask. To listen. To surrender. But be careful. God might tell you it's you who needs to change.

And here's the hard truth:

"For there is no partiality with God." Romans 2:11 (LSB)

He's not taking sides. He's after both of you. And He'll start wherever the heart is most willing.

Questions to ask yourself:

Where have I stopped fighting?

When's the last time I prayed with, not just for, my spouse?

What have I been expecting from them that I've stopped giving?

What's one way I can guard this marriage better this week?

Guarding what's sacred doesn't start with a grand gesture. It begins with one surrendered heart, one choice at a time.

Chapter 9

The Battleground: Your Purpose

What I Want to Be When I Grow Up

"For the gifts and the calling of God are irrevocable." Romans 11:29 (LSB)

Dreams Deferred

My mother had purchased a book to log or record things from my school years, beginning in kindergarten. No Pre-K in those days. It had school pictures and report cards. I'm still afraid to look at those. I noticed that every year, it had a list of things you wanted to be.

Funny, a CEO or business owner was never on the list—nor writer nor philosopher. But a cowboy, a policeman, a fireman, an Army guy, and a few others were there. At some point, I'm sure I checked most of them. A professional baseball player wasn't on the list either.

I did live in Oklahoma, so the cowboy thing was a given. I did join the Army, so I checked that box. I also served as a deputy sheriff so that I could check that box as well. But had I reached my dream?

According to my mother, when I was three, I wanted to grow up and be Lassie and have puppies. I'm so glad that dream did not come true. Not to mention the impossibilities on a couple of fronts there.

"I will give thanks to You, for I am fearfully and wonderfully made; Wonderful are Your works, And my soul knows it very well." Psalm 139:14 (LSB)

I don't know at what age we begin to dream of being big, of being older, taller, and able to do things on our own. Or at least try. I do remember when I added that "teen" to my age, visions of grandeur and fast cars began to swim around in my head. That's why my dad only let me have a Volkswagen Beetle. I got in enough trouble with it.

Wise man, my dad. I didn't think that back then. I still have friends today who laugh about my yellow VW bug in high school. I was lucky, I had friends who didn't have a car, and I could squeeze several into the backseat if we were careful.

I recall going to church camp every summer since I was around ten. And not once do I remember thinking I'd be a minister or pastor. I don't know if that was because it wasn't a dream or if I thought it would come later. Baseball, basketball, and dating were my things.

I figured I had time. And I'd never even heard the word 'legacy'.

Where were you when your dreams began to interrupt your days, your thoughts? Are you a daydreamer like I was in the sixth grade? Were they so big that just thinking about them could get you into trouble?

What were those dreams, and how big were they?

Time has a way of speeding up when you're not paying attention. One missed opportunity turns into five. One decision to delay becomes a decade. And if you're not careful, what once felt like purpose starts to feel like regret.

You start to wonder: *Did I miss it?*

Did I mishear God? Or was that just a dream I had, not a calling?

I remember sitting in a foxhole somewhere in Saudi Arabia, wondering if my time might run out. Everything in me thought maybe I had missed it. Had I run too far, waited too long, been broken too much? There wasn't a sign, no angel in the sky, just sand and heat.

But something happened. A man I didn't know sent me a Bible to read. He asked me to start with a Proverb every day and 6 chapters of Psalms. I would like to say God found me, but what happened was He met me where I was, in a foxhole.

I never got to meet that man, but his Bible saved me in the midst of the storm. I found out that even in my wildest dreams, I never would have thought God would come to meet me wherever I am, and I would be where I am today.

That gap, the one between what I thought life would be and where I actually landed, is the battleground.

When Dreams Get Quiet

The enemy doesn't need you to curse God to lose your purpose. He just needs you to settle. To compare. To reason. To believe that what you missed is greater than what God still wants to do.

He'll whisper things like:

"You're too late."
"You had your chance."
"Somebody else is already doing it better."

And little by little, your calling gets quieter. Not because God walked away. But because you did.

No fancy cars, no big houses, never played professional baseball, left college for the military, but I found God again in a foxhole. I truly don't think there are any atheists in foxholes. I never met one.

"The heart of man plans his way, but the Lord establishes his steps." Proverbs 16:9 (ESV)

Whether you are called to preach, teach, drive the church van, or welcome people at the door, God has purposed you there. God has given you that heart to stand where you are standing. In some cases, you aren't standing yet.

I know from firsthand experience that God never gives up on us. Never walks away from us, never doubts our ability, or loves us any less, even when we use his name in vain, get mad and yell at him, or blame him for what is going on in our lives.

God is bigger than any consequences we might endure and is the most intentional listener of any friend we will ever have. And that God longs to give us the desires of our hearts.

"Delight yourself in the Lord, and He will give you the desires of your heart." Psalm 37:4 (LSB)

I'm not talking about our selfish wishes and desires. I'm talking about being aligned with what we were designed for. When you delight in the Lord, your desires start to mirror His. That's when your calling gets real.

So let me ask you:

Where did your calling get quiet?
What did you dream before the world told you to be realistic?
Have you stopped asking God what He still wants to do through you?

You may not have become a pro athlete, CEO, or Lassie with puppies.
But that doesn't mean you missed it. It means God's not finished.

Because if you're still breathing, you're still called. And if you're still called, there's still a fight ahead.
Not to earn your worth, but to walk in your purpose.

How the Enemy Attacks Purpose

"For we are not ignorant of his schemes."
2 Corinthians 2:11 (LSB)

So, what are his schemes when it comes to your calling?

Most people assume the devil shows up with a pitchfork and some sin too big to ignore. But for those who've already surrendered their lives to Christ, the enemy changes his tactics. If he can't steal your salvation, he'll do everything he can to silence your purpose.

He doesn't always use sin to distract you. He uses comparison, delay, distraction, and discouragement. All of them feel justified. All of them feel like they make sense in the moment. But every one of them can cause a man or woman to lay down their calling quietly, with no fight at all.

Comparison

The enemy will let you love Jesus as long as you're too busy looking sideways to follow Him. You get so immersed in Bible study and other activities that you start looking around instead of up. Or you begin to think everyone else has figured it out. "She already wrote her book." "He's already preaching." They're doing what you thought you were supposed to do… it should have been you.

The lie? *"It should have been you."*

The truth? God is not limited by time and the order of things or who got there first.

After getting divorced, I started thinking I would never fulfill my calling. I was no longer qualified. I resigned myself to just being a member of a church. But God had other plans. He put me to work. I worked with the youth for a bit, drove the church van, picked up and dropped off children whose parents didn't come to church.

I actually shared my testimony with the youth one Sunday. I found out that one of those in attendance had an uncle who was the pastor from that revival so many years ago and had drawn that picture of a lighthouse with chalk.

Needless to say, the next time he came to town, we had a little reunion and a long talk. Our meeting again was an affirmation that I was again on the right track.

"Let us not become boastful, challenging one another, envying one another." – Galatians 5:26 (LSB)

Comparison wants you to believe your season is over. God says it's just getting started.

Delay

Sometimes the most spiritual-sounding trap is this one: *"You're not ready yet."* That voice that says:

"Get more training."

"Wait for the right time."

"You need someone else's permission."

"Don't step out until you're sure it'll work."

And while preparation has its place, there comes a time when waiting becomes disobedience. The Spirit says, "Go," but fear dresses up like wisdom and says, "Not yet."

I was working in a men's ministry here in Oklahoma. It was an outreach men's ministry meeting once a month on different weekends in different cities. I was told by the pastor leading it that all this driving was taking a toll, and he had asked the Lord to find someone to lead the group in Oklahoma City. God's answer was me!

My response. "Brother, let me tell you something. I don't speak in public, I don't pray in public, as a matter of fact, I don't even pray out loud!" Two weeks later, I found myself doing exactly all three of those things.

That pastor had told me, "Never tell God what you can or don't do."

"How long will you lie down, you lazy one? When will you arise from your sleep?" Proverbs 6:9 (LSB)

Delay sounds wise to you, but it is often just fear dressed up as wisdom.

Distraction

Not every distraction is sinful. Some look like good opportunities, but they're not your assignment. Maybe it's a job promotion that pays well but leads your heart away from ministry or takes up more of your time.

It could be serving in a place God never asked you to serve, and now you're exhausted and don't know why.

Have you ever found yourself volunteering for everyone else's vision and never saying yes to your own?

The enemy doesn't have to tempt you with failure if he can distract you with busyness.

There was a time when I was shooting to grow my savings and pay off some things. I had told my boss I would take every job he had coming up. I was gone a lot. I ended up not allowing any time at all for God. No daily routine, soon no more prayers. You just exist day by day for a better paycheck.

"Everything is permissible, but not everything is beneficial." 1 Corinthians 10:23 (NIV)

Discouragement

This one is sneaky because it uses your past against you. You tried something before, and it didn't work, or you classified it as a failure. You shared your story, and nobody responded. Maybe you tried to start a new group, and no one came back. You obeyed, but it didn't feel like it mattered. So, you stopped.

Not because God said stop. But because the results didn't match your expectations.

At the height of our ministry's success, we would reach 3,000 to 5,000 a day on social media with daily verses, prayers, and devotionals. When the pandemic changed, so did social media. In one day, those numbers were cut in half: the next week, half again. I blamed it on censorship. I blamed it on Satan. I wanted to give up.

I was angry, and I prayed. It was more complaint than prayer, honestly, questioning whether it was even worth it to keep posting verses and devotions every day. God used my own words to remind me of our purpose as a whole. To share.

I was reminded by Holy Spirit that I used to have a prayer every day that I put forth. It was, "Dear Lord, send me one today."

Holy Spirit then followed up by stating it wasn't my job to make sure the message was seen. It was my job to keep sending the message. Because faithfulness isn't measured by reach, it's measured by obedience.

"Therefore, my beloved brothers, be steadfast, immovable, always abounding in the work of the Lord, knowing that your labor is not in vain in the Lord."
1 Corinthians 15:58 (LSB)

The Whisper War

- You're too late.
- You missed your window.

- That wasn't really God.
- Someone else is doing it better.
- You're not holy enough.
- You messed up too much.

None of those voices comes from the Spirit. Not one.

Because if God gave the calling, then nothing, not age, not fear, not failure, can take it away. You may have gone quiet. But heaven hasn't.

So, where do you need to get back in the fight?

"Who saved us and called us to a holy calling, not because of our works but because of His own purpose and grace, which He gave us in Christ Jesus before the ages began." 2 Timothy 1:9 (ESV)

Walking In It

You don't have to strive for something God already gave you.

"So that you will walk in a manner worthy of the Lord, to please Him in all respects, bearing fruit in every good work and increasing in the knowledge of God." Colossians 1:10 (LSB)

That's the difference between purpose and performance.

When you begin walking in the anointing of your calling, it's not always easy, but there is always God's peace. You might feel the weight of your responsibility, but not the weight of anxiety.

Things can seem hard, but there's no heaviness feeling. You're no longer trying to impress people. You're simply trying to be faithful to the One who called you.

Doors begin to open that you never saw coming. Not because you went looking, but because God turned the handle. The work still costs something, but you no longer question whether it's worth it.

You're tired, but you're not empty. You pour it out, and somehow there's more to give. That's what walking in purpose feels like. Striving? That's a different beast entirely.

Striving is that constant pressure. Always questioning, always measuring. It looks like "ministry" or "hard work," but inside, you're not sure who you're really doing it for.

When you're striving, everything feels forced. You push and push, but nothing moves. You wonder why it feels off, but you keep going anyway because stopping would feel like failure.

You say things like, "I'm just being faithful," but what you're really doing is working yourself into the ground, waiting for fruit that never shows up.

The question isn't just: *Are you doing good things?* The question is: *Are you doing the right things?*

Start right here, where you are:
Obey God in the small things. Wake up. Be available.
Serve where you are.

So, what if you're still trying to figure out what you're here for? You don't need to know for the next ten years. You just need to say yes to the next ten minutes. Ask Him, "What do You want me to do today?" Then actually listen. And to be willing to move.

What makes you come alive?

What burden won't leave you alone?

What injustice keeps you up at night, or what need always catches your eye?

That's often where your calling starts. But don't wait for some sign from Holy Spirit. Most of the time, this clarity doesn't come until after the first step. It comes after.

So, here's the challenge:

- What's one step you can take this week toward your calling?
- Where have you been faithful that God might be preparing to expand?
- What burden won't leave you alone?
- Write these down in a journal, on a sticky note, but pray for them right now.

Purpose isn't proven in one big moment. It's revealed through obedience over time—a journey walked out in everyday life. One "yes," one act of faithfulness, one battle at a time. This is how you begin to walk in it. Are you ready?

"He has told you, mortal one, what is good; and what does the Lord require of you but to do justice, to love kindness, and to walk humbly with your God?" Micah 6:8 (LSB)

The only thing between where you are and what God called you to… is a step.
Will you take it?

Chapter 10

The Battleground: Your Children

Early Temptation, Identity Attacks, Generational Interference

If God gave you purpose, do you think the enemy will ignore your children until they're old enough to understand?

If he can't stop you from waking up to your calling, he'll aim for the ones watching you live it out. The best time to start chaos and confusion is while they are still young and don't have a voice.

"And these words that I command you today shall be on your heart. You shall teach them diligently to your children, and shall talk of them when you sit in your house, and when you walk by the way, and when you lie down, and when you rise." Deuteronomy 6:6–7 (ESV)

The Bloodline Battle

This is a battleground most men never knew existed, but they're in it whether they fight or not. Satan isn't just attacking your faith; he's trying to break your bloodline. Now, before you say I'm crazy, let's look at scripture first. Let's look at the cross of Jesus.

If the bloodline didn't matter, the enemy wouldn't be trying so hard to corrupt it, confuse it, or cut it off. But God doesn't just call people. The Father calls generations. If bloodlines didn't matter, Matthew wouldn't have opened his Gospel with 42 generations leading to Jesus. God was tracking something. And if He was tracking Jesus' bloodline, what do you think He's tracking in yours?

"Knowing that you were not redeemed with perishable things like silver or gold from your futile way of life inherited from your forefathers, but with precious blood, as of a lamb unblemished and spotless, the blood of Christ."
1 Peter 1:18–19 (LSB)

If bloodlines don't matter, why is there so much emphasis on Jesus spilling his blood for us, and why are there words like 'washed in the blood'?

"So all the generations from Abraham to David were fourteen generations, and from David to the deportation to Babylon fourteen generations, and from the deportation to Babylon to the Christ fourteen generations."
Matthew 1:17 (ESV)

Your bloodline matters too. In more ways than we know. If God tracked 42 generations to get to Jesus, what do you think He's trying to birth through you? If God is tracking your family's generations, guess who else is, too?

What you ignore, your children may inherit. This is the point in time. . . in your life that you need to ask yourself some serious questions.

Questions like:

- "What am I passing down"?
- "What war am I ignoring that my kids are inheriting"?
- "What blessing has God been trying to restore through my obedience?"
- What blessing is my family or my children missing because of my disobedience"?

"You shall not worship them nor serve them; for I, the Lord your God, am a jealous God, inflicting the punishment of the fathers on the children, even to the third and fourth generations of those who hate Me, but showing favor to thousands, to those who love Me and keep My commandments." Exodus 20:5–6 (LSB)

The enemy isn't just after your "today". He's after your tomorrow, your family name, your legacy.
But God has already written a better story.

There are consequences in what is passed down—old habits, agreements, patterns, and spiritual strongholds.

Scripture doesn't hide that. But the idea that your father's sins doom you is not the gospel.

"The person who sins will die. A son will not suffer the punishment for the father's guilt, nor will a father suffer the punishment for the Son's guilt; the righteousness of the righteous will be upon himself, and the wickedness of the wicked will be upon himself." Ezekiel 18:20 (LSB)

So, here's the truth: You're not cursed by your father's sins, but you may inherit their patterns until someone stands up and breaks them.

God may allow the pattern to play out *until someone stands up and breaks it*. And that someone might be you.

There may be generational curses that run to the third and fourth generation, but mercy runs to the thousandth. Don't just break the cycle; replace it with God's blessing.

The enemy may have run through your family's history... but in Jesus, now so can faithfulness.

Father and mother wounds inside silent homes are some of the most successful strategies against us. Today's war is waged through media, distraction, isolation, and distorted identity. If we, as parents, fall asleep and become numb to the world, our children grow up numb and unarmed. You are not just a father or mother; you are a gatekeeper!

How the Enemy Targets Children

"When I saw their fear, I stood and said to the nobles, the officials, and the rest of the people, 'Do not be afraid of them; remember the Lord who is great and awesome, and fight for your brothers, your sons, your daughters, your wives, and your houses.'" Nehemiah 4:14 (LSB)

The enemy doesn't wait until your children grow up to the age of accountability. Darkness does not wait to go to war against them. Evil has no mercy; it starts early. Because if he can twist their view of the world, or worse, their view of themselves, he doesn't have to wait for them to fail in life.

They'll self-destruct before they ever step into their calling. This isn't new. Satan has been doing this since the garden.

It just looks different now.

Early Temptation

Temptation doesn't wait for adulthood. It starts young. What used to take time, and curiosity now shows up in the palm of their hand. The world knows it doesn't have to take your children out with violence. It can seduce them with convenience. With popularity on social media.

What once came through the back doors of our families now comes through Wi-Fi. What once took effort to find now shows up in ads, apps, and explorer and Google pages. And it's not just sexual temptation. It's a dopamine addiction. It's scrolling until you feel numb. It's chasing affirmation from people you'll never meet.

The screen in their pocket is a doorway. And if you're not guarding it, someone else is using it.

Recently, my granddaughter refused to stop playing video games with an online friend. I repeated myself, and she still refused. I had to explain that if she didn't turn it off, I would, and she wouldn't like my way. She seemed to understand that.

But here's what hit me in that moment: I had to guard my own heart just as much as hers. I was tempted to get angry, to yell, and to punish her for arguing. I had to choose to keep my voice calm. Because while our children are being tempted and influenced, so are we. The battle isn't just for them. It's in us too.

Is it temptation or influence for a child to know instinctively that they don't want to share? If you can remember being very young, did you ever plot to steal just one more cookie? Plot? I had already planned the excuse as well! All children test boundaries, but do they become a persistent pattern? I'm not saying everything is evil or influenced by dark forces. But what I am saying is this: Patterns of behavior can be used later and influenced by dark forces.

Identity Attacks

If the enemy can confuse their identity, he can rewrite their destiny. That's always been the plan: to attack the image of God by distorting the image they see in the mirror.

We used to ask, "What do you want to be when you grow up?" Now we're asking, "What are you?"

Gender confusion.

Victim mentality.

Entitlement and insecurity are weaponized through comparison.

It begins in the form of quiet self-hatred. Feeling like they'll never measure up. Watching perfectly curated lives on social media and believing everyone else is winning . . . just not them.

The devil loves to use delay as a sign of unanswered prayer.

Remind your children of these things:

Their identity is not up for debate.
God does not make mistakes.
It was written in heaven before they ever took their first breath.

What they may want right now, they may have to wait for. But God will come through for them.

"Before I formed you in the womb I knew you, and before you were born I consecrated you." – Jeremiah 1:5 (LSB)

Generational Patterns Repeating

If Satan can't create, he'll recycle. That's what generational curses are. Cycles the enemy wants to repeat. Anger, addiction, passivity, pride. He'll dress them up differently, but the root stays the same. What wasn't healed in you, he'll try to hand it to your children.

That's why parenting is more than behavior management. It's spiritual warfare. Because you're not just raising kids. You're building a legacy. And if you don't fight for it, the enemy will *claim* it by default.

Before I began to raise my children in church, I was an angry man. I was a broken man. The day everything turned around was one Saturday morning after fixing my children's breakfast. There was a napkin on the floor, and I asked my son to pick it up. It was directly behind him as he stood talking to me in the kitchen.

He turned around, but it was so close he stepped over it, and now it was behind him again. After two doses of watching this play out, I began to yell. After two more, I grabbed the closest thing to me to throw, and it was a pan of bacon grease. Don't worry, I missed my target.

While we were both wiping down the wall and cleaning up my mess. I told both of them, "Tomorrow we're going to find a church." We never looked back. I did not want to pass that anger on to my son or my daughter.

As embarrassing as that is to tell, guess who I learned that from? My father. I tried to go back in history to find the root cause of such uncontrollable anger. I had never seen my grandfather lose his temper. Nor any of my uncles. Did it start with my dad? Regardless, I made sure it was going to end with me.

What You Don’t Fight For, You Lose

You can’t just pray for your children; you have to war for them. When you do pray for them, you don't just ask for protection and guidance; you declare it over them.

Don't just do this in silence. Pray in front of them. Fight this battle in front of them so they know you are fighting, and they learn to fight for themselves. Have you ever prayed over your children this way? Have you ever heard of anyone praying over their children this way?

Here is an example:

Father, thank you for my family for this great gift you have given me. Today, Father, I declare in the name of Jesus that in this house your kingdom reigns. That the blood of Jesus covers this place. No darkness or evil shall enter in to interrupt or influence the hearts and minds of our children. Our marriage. I decree this home as yours, the family is yours, and you are welcome here at all times. Father, when my children leave here, I declare a hedge of protection around them as if they were safe in our home, safe in your presence, dear Lord. This day and every day. In Jesus' name, Amen.

Pray over their mind, not just their body.

Speak life over their identity, not just correction for their behavior.

Keep watch when they're too tired to.

You're not just their provider.

You're their intercessor.

Their protector.

You are their first picture of what spiritual covering looks like.

This is about more than rules and routines. It is way more than just prayer discipline. It's about repentance. About standing in the gap and saying, "It stops with me."

It's not about being perfect. It's about being present.

About refusing to hand your children over to culture by default.

About repenting for what you didn't know, and then fighting like they're going to hell for what matters now. Because they might if you don't!

"But the lovingkindness of the LORD is from everlasting to everlasting on those who fear Him, And His righteousness to children's children, To those who keep His covenant And remember His precepts to do them."
Psalm 103:17–18 (LSB)

Arrows in the Quiver

Children are not meant just to be protected but aimed. Not shielded from spiritual warfare, but they are the very arrows in the quiver. Shaped, sharpened, and launched. We should prepare them to walk with the Spirit so they can shape the next generation.

"Behold, children are a gift of the Lord, The fruit of the womb is a reward. Like arrows in the hand of a warrior, So are the children of one's youth." Psalm 127:3–4 (LSB)

Like arrows in the hands of a warrior, that's what Scripture says. And a warrior doesn't just admire his arrows. He trains with them. Sharpens them. Learns their weight. Then, at the right moment, he releases them with direction and intent.

The world would love for you to believe your only job as a parent is to protect your kids. Keep them safe. Keep them quiet. Keep them entertained.

But Scripture says your job is not just to shield them, it's to aim them.

That means you don't just prepare them for success. You prepare them for battle.

You teach them how to hear the voice of God.

You show them how to repent quickly and forgive often. You let them see you worship. You let them see you wrestle.

They don’t need perfection. They need an example.

An example doesn’t come from lectures; it comes from being a witness to it in your life. When do you teach your children spiritual discipline? Maybe at the dinner table, blessing the food and talking about your day?

I believe it's the best place to learn from them. I used to take my children to their favorite Mexican restaurant. Once the food came, their brains clicked off, and oh, the wonders of their days spilled out like water from a spring. We learned to talk about everything, anything, at dinner. We learned to share with each other. That is discipleship.

When do you train them to fight spiritual battles? On the drive to school? How do you react in traffic when someone cuts you off?

Do you pray over their friendships and their thoughts?

When do you show them what forgiveness looks like? Right after you blow it? Can you come back and say, “I was wrong. Will you forgive me?”

Training happens in the ordinary. It doesn’t need a schedule. It needs intentionality. It needs discernment. And it needs your attention, even when you're tired.

And when the time comes, and it will, you must accept you won't be able to shield them from every attack. But you have the ability to show them where to run. Who to trust. What it looks like to stand firm.

So, ask yourself:

- Am I raising protectors or bystanders in the kingdom?
- Am I training my children to stand on truth or just to duck their heads and give in?
- Where in our daily life could I be more intentional spiritually?

You can't control the winds of change they'll face. But you can control how you shape the arrow.
You can choose to aim them toward faith, not fear, towards legacy, not silence.

So, start where you are. Teach what you know. Pray as you go.
And fight for their future like their lives depend on it because they do.

What are you launching into the world? Fear or faithfulness? Silence or legacy?

Father, let me be the one who stands in the gap for my children and the next generation. Let me be faithful when others run. Let me see and hear the lies before they even try to settle into their hearts and minds. Let me guard what Holy Spirit has given me and train up the arrows You've placed in my quiver. In Jesus' name, Amen.

"Train up a child in the way he should go; even when he grows older, he will not abandon it." Proverbs 22:6 (LSB)

Chapter 11

The Armor You Never Knew You Had

You've seen the battlegrounds: your mind, your marriage, your purpose, and your children. Now let me show you what you're already wearing.

You're not just a survivor in this spiritual war. You're a soldier. You're already standing in a place of victory. God hasn't saved you so that you can sit on the sidelines. He's armed you.

The problem isn't your lack of strength or skill. It's your failure to accept and recognize the weapons in your hands.

What if I told you the fight you feel unprepared for, God has already equipped you to face?

What if it's already inside you?

What if it surrounds you?

God never designed us to go through this life to simply exist, but to reign with Him.

Understanding the armor is only the first step. Putting it on daily, living it out, is where the fight is won. Many of us who've walked hard roads testify to the power of making a daily habit of putting on the armor of God each morning.

It's more than routine; it's a declaration of readiness, a spiritual preparation for the battles ahead. Not because we're perfect or fearless, but because the fight never stops.

"But in all these things we overwhelmingly conquer through Him who loved us." Romans 8:37 (LSB)

A Knight in Shining Armor

When I was a teen, I remember hearing girls talk about their "knight in shining armor." Back then, I thought it was just romance. Now I realize it was something deeper, a longing for someone strong enough to fight for what matters. The only biblical story I knew about armor back then was David and Goliath. King Saul tried to make David wear his armor, which was way too heavy for him. But David had on God's armor; they didn't see it. Neither did Goliath before he fell.

You may have heard this story used to decorate sermons or Sunday school lessons. But this armor isn't decoration. It's power. It's gear for the real fight, your everyday battles.

So, if you were a soldier or a knight in God's army, what part of your armor would you put on first? What does the scripture tell us to put on first?

"Therefore take up the whole armor of God, that you may be able to withstand in the evil day, and having done all, to stand firm. Stand therefore, having fastened on the belt of truth, and having put on the breastplate of righteousness." Ephesians 6:13–14 (LSB)

The Belt of Truth

Why would you suppose we would want to gird our waist with a belt of truth first? Paul is instructing us to *put on the belt of truth first*, just like a soldier would wrap a belt tightly around his waist to secure all other armor pieces to it. But why?

In the military, those straps you see over those soldiers' arms that are connected to their belt, which has several other attachments, are called an LBE. It stands for, or it used to be, "Load Bearing Equipment." It is the centerpiece that holds things together. It supports the load.

Secondly, how hard will you fight for something you not only love but believe in with all your heart?

You know our military men and women joined out of patriotism for their country. But their willingness to die is because they believe in it. They believe in those next to them whom they have learned to trust. It's about the relationships we have that give us the willingness to die for someone else, our brothers, our families, for our children, as Jesus did for the world.

"Greater love has no one than this: to lay down one's life for one's friends." John 15:13 (NIV)

The Breastplate of Righteousness

Jesus spoke of this kind of love, one that calls for more than courage. It demands righteousness, guarding our hearts and motivations. And that's what the breastplate does: it protects what is most vulnerable, but also that fire that beats inside of us. What is righteousness? It's our heart posture when we are in alignment with God's holiness and purpose for us. It's living in a way or fighting really hard to live in a way that reflects His character and purposes, so that they are seen in us.

"Watch over your heart with all diligence, For from it flow the springs of life." Proverbs 4:23 (LSB)

The Shoes for Our Feet

The Greek word translated as "preparation" is ἑτοιμασία (hetoimasia), which means readiness or a firm foundation. You don't need shoes to stand; you need them to walk, to step out onto the sidewalks and roads purposeful with the gospel of Jesus planted in your heart. You don't need shoes to wait on a miracle; you need them to help create them.

"and having shod your feet with the preparation of the gospel of peace." Ephesians 6:15 (LSB)

The enemy wants you stuck or standing still, paralyzed by your own fears or doubts. But these shoes are made for walking, for moving forward. For carrying the word of God with peace into the fight. For planting the seeds of salvation on every kind of soil you come across, even when the ground's rough.

The Shield of Faith

Just as I envision the breastplate like a bulletproof vest, I can see the shield as well. The big difference here is that it can be wielded by either hand, can be carried, placed in front, behind, to the sides, and above me.

"In all circumstances take up the shield of faith, with which you can extinguish all the flaming darts of the evil one." Ephesians 6:16 (ESV)

It is defensive in nature, but I can use it to push my way through as well. It is an extension of my movement, it protects, and it propels.

I also see it as the cover behind which I can rest, while breaking the arrows of lies the world shoots my way continuously. That is faith. That is God. Standing in front, beside, behind, a strong tower, and a friend.

"You hem me in, behind and before, and lay your hand upon me." Psalm 139:5 (ESV)

The Helmet of Salvation

The helmet of salvation is one of the final pieces you place upon your body. But why a helmet of salvation? It isn't just about a one-time salvation event or simply the place where you made a decision.

This helmet is to protect your thoughts from the lies of condemnation, fear, and doubt.

"And take the helmet of salvation, and the sword of the Spirit, which is the word of God." Ephesians 6:17 (LSB)

This helmet covers your head on every side and on top for those blows you don't see coming. It reminds you who you are in Christ, a redeemed son, called and now covered. All your defenses are now in place. The helmet guards your mind, the place where the battle often begins.

Salvation is the result of your faith and belief in Jesus.

Your willingness to act, to step forward and proclaim yourself a child of God. The helmet merely secures your mind so you can think clearly, stand firm, stay focused on what's ahead without the fear of what's behind, and keep marching forward when the enemy tries to rattle your confidence or steal your hope.

This helmet should remind you that you belong to God, you are redeemed, and nothing can separate you from that salvation.

"For I am convinced that neither death, nor life, nor angels, nor principalities, nor things present, nor things to come, nor powers, nor height, nor depth, nor any other created thing, will be able to separate us from the love of God, which is in Christ Jesus our Lord."
Romans 8:38–39 (LSB)

Why Did David Not Need Armor?

We read in *1 Samuel 17:38–39,* when King Saul tried to put his armor on David before facing Goliath, David refused. Why? It didn't fit! Saul's armor was heavy, unfamiliar, and restrictive for David, a shepherd boy used to agility and reliance on God, not the physical battle gear made by men.

David's confidence came from his *relationship* with God, not from man-made armor. His "helmet" was his faith and salvation, his trust in the Lord's protection and power.

Armor made with human hands can weigh you down if it's not yours or you're not trained to wear it. David moved freely with a sling and stones; those were the weapons God had equipped him with.

What heavy, or man-made, armor are you carrying today that slows you down or holds you back? That armor of tradition, of religion, or personal preference.

Maybe it's armor that isn't yours, or perhaps it was passed down from generation to generation, and now you try to carry all those scars as well.

What would it look like to trust fully in the helmet of salvation God has offered to you to walk free, confident, and ready with the weapons He's equipped you to wield?

"Thus says the LORD of hosts, 'If you will walk in My ways, and if you will keep My charge, then you shall also judge My house, and you shall also keep My courts, and I will give you free access among these who stand here.'" Zechariah 3:7 (LSB)

The Sword of the Spirit: The Word of God

The sword is the only true offensive weapon in your armor. Every other piece is defense for holding ground, protecting your heart and mind. But the sword? The sword is your power to strike back. It is what God has given all of us to prepare us step by step.

". . . and the sword of the Spirit, which is the word of God." Ephesians 6:17 (LSB)

This sword is not a blunt object. It's a razor-sharp weapon, and in God's power, alive and active (Hebrews 4:12). This sword isn't meant to kill human beings; it's meant to save them. (John 3:17, 2 Corinthians 2:16) It cuts through lies, fear, doubt, and every fiery dart the enemy hurls your way.

The sword isn't just words written on a page. It's the *Rhema Word*—the '*Word of God* spoken out loud, declared in faith, and wielded in battle. When Jesus faced the enemy in the wilderness (Matthew 4:1–11, Luke 4:1–13) after fasting for 40 days and 40 nights, He didn't argue or debate; He didn't try to be right. He spoke the Word, not out of hate or anger, but out of love. That's your model. This is the sword that lays low the power of the enemy.

What lies do you need to cut down today? What doubts, fears, or accusations are slashing at your confidence? What moments in your past keep coming back time and time again to haunt you, to condemn you? This sword is for those moments.

When the lie comes: 'You're a terrible parent,' cut it down with: *'I am who God says I am, and He's making me more like Him every day.'* (2 Corinthians 3:18)

When the accusation comes: 'You'll never be free from that sin,' strike back with: *'Whom the Son sets free is free indeed.'* (John 8:36)

But here's the catch: the sword only works if it's in your hands. It's not enough to carry the Word; you have to wield it. Speak it, declare it, and claim it. Shout it from the rooftops if need be.

The enemy hates it when people begin to read the Word. He fears it. Because where the Word is wielded in faith, strongholds fall (2 Corinthians 10:3-5, James 4:7), condemnation becomes salvation, shame turns into redemption, and hate loses out to love. So, stand firm. Hold your shield. Guard your heart and mind.

But never forget, your fight. . . the sword wins the battle. You were not chosen just to survive. You were chosen to be an heir to the kingdom of God, a royal priest, a son or daughter. You were chosen to stand and to strike.

"But thanks be to God, who gives us the victory through our Lord Jesus Christ. Therefore, my beloved brethren, be steadfast, immovable, always abounding in the work of the Lord, knowing that your toil is not in vain in the Lord."
1 Corinthians 15:57–58 (LSB)

What part of your armor do you tend to leave on the ground? Is it truth? Righteousness? Peace? Faith? The Word? The helmet that reminds you who you are? Ask the Spirit to show you.

Don't pick it up in shame. Pick it up on purpose. You were never meant to fight this battle naked. You were meant to be armed in grace.

"Put on the full armor of God, so that you will be able to stand firm against the schemes of the devil."
Ephesians 6:11 (LSB)

Prayer – Already Armed

Father, remind me that I am already armed with Your sword. I don't have to have every word memorized to do battle; all I need is what You have placed on my heart and in my spirit.

Help me pick up anything I've dropped or failed to use properly. Show me where I've been fighting without my sword and not in truth.

Give me the strength to stand when everything in this world screams sit down. Give me peace at all times, help me to rejoice in all things.

Help me hear Holy Spirit, especially when my armor is on Father. I ask all of this in Jesus' Holy name, Amen.

Chapter 12

The Cost of the Cross

Jesus didn't promise safety. He promised the Cross.

Have you ever wondered what it is that wakes you up in the middle of the night, at 3 a.m.? How often do you roll over and flip your pillow to the cool side and go back to sleep?

Were you awakened from a dream, or jolted by something else in a dream, or a noise in the night?

"Behold, I stand at the door and knock; if anyone hears My voice and opens the door, I will come in to him and will dine with him, and he with Me." Revelation 3:20 (LSB)

For me at least, it seems God loves 3 a.m., and if I listen and don't try to go back to sleep, I can hear Him. "I'm here. Wake up." It feels like God is saying, "I've got something to say, but I didn't want to interrupt your day, so I woke you up to give you enough time to talk before you need to get up and go to work."

"I'm here, waiting quietly beside your restless night. Can you hear me? I have something for your heart before the sun rises." God doesn't plead with me like that, but I hear me telling myself that because that sounds so much better.

Sometimes the cost of the Cross is waking up at 3 a.m. Not because you can't sleep, but because God won't let you. He interrupts your rest because He has something to say that can't wait. And when you finally answer that knock at the door, you realize: the cost isn't what you give up. The cost is what happens when you don't.

Is There a Cost? A Sacrifice?

Why Do I Need to Give Up Everything?

If your Christianity doesn't cost you anything, are you really following Jesus?

Here's the truth: it will cost you something. Your time. Your comfort. Your old way of living. Maybe even relationships with people who don't understand why you changed. But what you're calling a "cost" might not be what you think it is.

What did the Cross ask of Jesus?
What will the Cross ask of you?

I can say that the gospel of Jesus demands the Cross, not comfort. But what does that really mean? To be honest, it may be different for you than for me. We each bear our own Cross, our own struggles, and our own burdens. But we don't have to do it alone.

"Then he called the crowd to join his disciples and said, 'If any of you wants to be my follower, you must give up your own way, take up your Cross daily, and follow me. If you try to hang on to your life, you will lose it. But if you give up your life for my sake and for the sake of the Good News, you will save it." Mark 8:34-35 (NLT)

I believe Mark 8:34-35 tells us exactly what the cost is. If we want to hang on to or keep doing things the same way, it will lead to death. But if we give up that life and follow Him, for his sake and the news that Jesus died and rose again to conquer sin and death, then we will live an eternal life.

The Real Cost

At the beginning of this journey, we can even use my journey if you like. I thought I had time. Maybe I did. But what did running from God actually cost me?

I really had to stop looking at it in this way. What did it cost me? What did it cost those closest to me? How did I behave or react in ways that made things worse instead of better because I was trying to fight all my battles on my own?

What did it cost? A moment that might have made a difference in someone else's life. Time not wasted chasing wealth and not seeing how much I already had.

In my late twenties, after leaving the military, I threw myself into building my life. I had come home and reconnected with a girl I had grown up with. She became my wife soon after.

I told myself I needed to be providing, that every hour at work or buried in paperwork was more important. But really, I was chasing something else, approval, maybe? Appreciation? Certainly, love and a sense of worth.

I measured my value in titles or if my life aligned with my dreams. God was calling me even then, but I drowned Him out with work, playing golf, or going fishing. I ignored the Father due to the focus of my own ambition.

It's strange how sin can disguise itself as "responsibility."

I wasn't in bars or running the streets. I was the guy who always said yes to everything else. I was the one who showed up early and left late. And in the process, I wasn't leading my family to God. I was ignoring them like I was God.

That's what the cost of running from God really was: missed opportunities to love people well. Broken trust. Silent dinners. Kids who grew up learning that work came before them. And yet, when I finally surrendered, when I stopped clinging to the version of "success" the world has placed on me and let God define my worth, something shifted. My priorities changed. My heart softened. I started showing up. It was slow and imperfect, but healing began.

I used to think following Jesus meant losing everything. Now I see it was the only way to get back what mattered most.

And here's the hard lesson I learned over time: what I thought was costing me everything stopped feeling like a cost at all.

Those early mornings I spent in prayer? They have become the best part of my day. The time I spent discipling my kids instead of being gone all the time for work? Those became the moments I treasured most. Those so-called "sacrifices" I made to follow Jesus? They became the very things that brought me the most joy.

Paul said it this way in Philippians 3:8, everything he once counted as gain, he now counted as loss compared to knowing Christ. Not because he was miserable, but because knowing Jesus was so much better that everything else looked like garbage in comparison.

The cost didn't disappear. But it faded in the light of His glory.

"More than that, I count all things to be loss because of the surpassing value of knowing Christ Jesus my Lord, for

whom I have suffered the loss of all things, and count them but rubbish so that I may gain Christ."
Philippians 3:8 (LSB)

In comparison, what I would have gained had I not run from God would far outweigh any cost I might have paid, but it never felt like I did.

What I finally understood and began to see evidence in my life: the cost wasn't what I gave up when I followed Jesus. The cost was everything I lost while I was running from Him.

When I say cost, I don't mean anything of monetary value. I mean losing relationships with family and with my children. I mean, missing those moments of laughter and joy you get from coming home every day to a child greeting you at the door. Instead of being a mom or dad, you're merely their biological father or mother.

So, before we step off into our selfish ambitions and desires and begin measuring costs, figure out the costs if you start putting others first before yourself.

If you start loving God even a fraction as much as He loves you. Allowing that love to become something more than a feeling or emotion, but a purpose. If you're willing to risk it all for someone else, to open your heart and let God in—then He can share His heart through you.

"Do nothing from selfish ambition or conceit, but in humility count others more significant than yourselves." Philippians 2:3 (ESV)

What Jesus Really Promised

What did Jesus actually promise?
Not health, wealth, and prosperity. Not a comfortable life. Not safety from suffering.

Jesus promised that if you follow Him, meaning if you walk in His footsteps, carry your burdens, and nail them to the Cross on which He died for all sin for all time, then you die on that Cross with Jesus.

This leads to healing the wounds of this world. It begins with allowing yourself to give up all those past pains, hurts, arguments, sins, fits of anger, hate, jealousy, envy, frustration, and depression.

Rising again out of the depths of the hell you were living in, washed as white as snow. Those chains and bruises are gone, and the sins of this world are gone as far as the east is from the west.

Rejoice! You've completed step 1. You've died and risen in Jesus Christ.

"As far as the east is from the west, so far does he remove our transgressions from us." Psalm 103:12 (ESV)

The gospel of Jesus Christ is a call to die to self, not just believing in a name. It's surrendering, giving up control, letting go of pain, but also embracing it. When we follow in His footsteps with the same authority and power given to us through the Holy Spirit, it doesn't remove the temptations and attacks or ridicule that Jesus endured as well. It takes faith and obedience.

Faith is waking up tired, worn down by the fight, wanting to hit the snooze button, and still deciding to step into the battle again. Obedience means picking up the Cross from the day before when your heart is heavy, and your past mistakes are shouting louder than your future hope. It's messy. It's hard. But it's where life and power begin.

To embrace pain is to surrender your right to comfort and control. It's saying to God, "Use this brokenness. Make me new." The gospel calls us to die to ourselves, and that often means dying to comfort, to ease, and sometimes even to our plans.

Real discipleship isn't comfortable Christianity. It's not 'say a prayer, and you're good.' It may cost everything, but in the end, it gives you everything in return.

"Go therefore and make disciples of all nations, baptizing them in the name of the Father and of the Son and of the Holy Spirit, teaching them to observe all that I have

commanded you. And behold, I am with you always, to the end of the age." Matthew 28:19-20 (ESV)

The gospel calls us to death and freedom from sin and leads to a new life filled with power and purpose. Salvation is not a call to comfort, but a call to commitment, to a covenant with the Father.

As we begin to walk in the footsteps of Jesus, we begin to embrace the Cross daily and to make disciples who do the same.

Any Cost Fades in His Glory

So yes, there is a cost. The cost is real. Daily surrender. Obedience when it's hard. Waking up at 3 a.m. when God knocks. Choosing His way over yours.

But here's what happens when you actually pick up your Cross and follow Him: the cost starts to fade.

What felt like sacrifice at first becomes an inheritance. What looked like loss becomes gain. The burden you thought would crush you becomes light. Not because it gets easier, but because His presence makes it worth it.

The early mornings stop feeling like interruptions and start feeling like appointments with the King. The time you spend in prayer stops feeling like obligation and starts feeling like oxygen. The "sacrifices" you make stop looking and feeling like loss and start growing like the best investment you ever made.

You stop counting what you gave up and start counting what you gained. You stop mourning what you lost and start celebrating what you found. You realize you didn't lose anything ...you exchanged it. Your burden for His. Your way for His way. Your life for His life.

"For I consider that the sufferings of this present time are not worthy to be compared with the glory that is to be revealed to us." Romans 8:18 (LSB)

When you're walking in His glory, living in His power, experiencing His presence daily, the cost? It looks like nothing.

The Cross has a cost, and Jesus paid it. But the glory that follows? It makes every perceived sacrifice worth it.

And then some.

Chapter 13

Grace That Becomes Power

In Weakness and Suffering

I had to go look up the word grace once, and not very long ago. I wanted to check my definition because forgiveness (grace) was very difficult for me in that season.

This is what the dictionary had to say:

Grace (noun)

1. a: unmerited divine assistance given humans for their regeneration or sanctification.
   b: a virtue coming from God.

2. a: disposition to or an act or instance of kindness, courtesy, or clemency
   b: a state of sanctification enjoyed through divine grace.

Unmerited? Doesn't that mean undeserved? *Unmerited* means you don't earn it, don't deserve it, yet it's freely given anyway. That's the *beauty and the sting* of grace at the same time. It's God's kindness toward us when we're most broken, weak, and definitely most undeserving. Not because of what we've done, but because of who He is.

That's a tough truth for a lot of us to swallow. It was tough for me, too. Especially when forgiveness feels impossible or when we're wrestling with our own failures, our own hurt feelings, and wounds. But grace is what breaks chains, knocks down walls, and turns hate into love, not condemnation.

So, Isn't That Forgiveness?

Yes, grace *is* forgiveness, but it's more than just wiping the slate clean. Grace is the unearned, undeserved kindness and mercy God shows us, forgiving our sins not because we deserve it, but because of His love and mercy. Forgiveness is part of grace; it's God choosing to release us from the debt of sin.

But grace also carries power to heal, restore, and strengthen us in our weakness. It's the bridge from brokenness to new life. So, when you say grace, you're talking about forgiveness *and* the supernatural power that flows from it. This kind turns weakness into strength, failure into a platform, and suffering into a breakthrough.

"My grace is sufficient for you, for My power is made perfect in weakness." 2 Corinthians 12:9 (NIV)

Are mercy and kindness a part of grace, too? What are those exactly?

Mercy and kindness are the heartbeats of grace, each with a slightly different focus but all intertwined:

Mercy is God *not giving us the punishment we deserve*. It's holding back judgment and extending compassion when we've messed up. It's like a judge who says, "I could punish you for your crimes, but I won't."

Kindness is God *actively doing good to us, even when we don't deserve it*. It's the loving actions and care that flow out of His heart. It's like the judge who not only drops the charges but also gives you a helping hand to rebuild your life.

Put it all together, and "*grace"* is God's *unearned* love, mercy (withholding punishment), kindness (giving goodness), and forgiveness (removing the debt) all wrapped up in one. That's the power we need to learn to lean into when the world and life break us down.

You said you wanted to follow Jesus, so let's show some grace to those who don't deserve it.

I actually growled at God when He first told me that. Not a literal growl, but you know the feeling—that internal resistance that rises up when you know God's right, but you don't want Him to be. Because of showing grace to people who hurt you? That's asking a lot.

But here's what I learned: if I don't show grace, I become the prisoner.

So, what happens if I don't show grace or forgiveness?

You stay chained to the person who hurt you. Unforgiveness is a prison where you're both the inmate and the guard. You replay the hurt. You rehearse what you should have said. You imagine revenge. And all the while, the person who wounded you is living their life while you're trapped reliving the pain.

Jesus said it plainly: if you don't forgive others, your Father won't forgive you. Not because God is petty, but because unforgiveness closes your heart to receiving the very grace you desperately need.

The Requirement to Forgive

Who am I supposed to forgive? Everyone.

The ones who hurt you the most. Your father, mother, friends, maybe even yourself. Anyone who broke your trust or left you feeling abandoned and alone. Forgiveness isn't about excusing sin or pretending it didn't happen. It's about releasing them from the debt they owe you, so you're no longer a prisoner, and you're no longer trying to make them one.

"For if you forgive others their trespasses, your heavenly Father will also forgive you; but if you do not forgive others, neither will your Father forgive your trespasses." Matthew 6:14–15 (ESV)

Forgiveness is no longer an option. If we try to reduce it or pick and choose, the enemy will hand it back to us on a platter. It's the heartbeat of the gospel. Without it, we're still chained.

And maybe that's where you are right now, sitting in the wreckage, wondering if grace is even possible.

Grace in the Wreckage

Chances are, you've experienced the results of a divorce or breakup in your family. You could be sitting somewhere right now, angry at the world, blaming yourself, or others for where you are in this moment.

There might be guards at the end of the hallway or on the other side of that locked gate in prison. There are hundreds, if not thousands, of reasons you find yourself amidst the wreckage we sometimes experience in our lives.

But when we find grace, when we are shown grace from God, we see that it doesn't ignore the wreckage. It doesn't pretend our pain isn't there or that sin doesn't matter.

Grace *shows up* in the lonely places, the cold, dark shadows, the unanswered prayers. Grace is choosing to love when love feels absent, just like Christ loves His church when it became rebellious and broken, when they hung Him on a cross.

"Now before the feast of the Passover, Jesus knowing that His hour had come to depart from this world to the Father, having loved His own who were in the world, He loved them to the end." John 13:1 (LSB)

I know because I've been there. I think that the majority of us have been there, and some may still be there. Those sleepless nights filled with anger and frustration, when I wanted to walk away but stayed because obedience whispered, *"This is part of the cross you carry."* Grace taught me that loving someone who doesn't love me back the way I want isn't weakness; it is strength forged in the fire of surrender.

This grace isn't a free pass for us to continue in sin. It exposes it. It calls it out. But it also shines a light on a new hope we can cling to. The kind of hope that God can heal, restore, and remake even the most shattered of hearts.

If you're carrying this kind of brokenness, I'm not telling you to fake it till you make it. I'm inviting you to step into grace. To tell God, "I'm messy, I'm broken and tired, and I need your love and powerful grace." I *need* the same grace that raised Christ from His grave that frees my mind, body, spirit, and soul to keep fighting even when I'm tired.

There was a season when grace felt like the last thing I wanted to give. I had every "right" to hold on to anger, or so I thought. Years ago, someone close to me gave up on me and walked away. It wasn't a single moment of hurt but a thousand little cuts that bled out over the next few years. Words said that left me hopeless. Every part of me felt like an anchor on a sinking ship.

I carried that for years. Let it harden into bitterness. I told myself I was justified.

Then, more recently, I found myself in the same place with someone else, and I told God flat out, "I don't want to forgive them. They don't deserve it." Soon after, while attending a leadership conference that turned out to be more than that, I learned a new definition of forgiveness. "To give like before." To give the same love, respect, encouragement, joy, peace, and honor like I did before the hurt, the pain, the loss—the way God forgives. Like before, we even committed those sins.

Forgiveness didn't free them that night; it freed me. That's what grace does. It doesn't erase the wreckage, but it plants a seed of resurrection right there in the ashes.

The gospel isn't comfortable, not because it doesn't want to be, but because God meets us where we're at, and that is rarely comfortable. It is our cross to bear, but not alone. By relying on Jesus, the Holy Spirit gives us the strength and the power to carry it.

"The Spirit of the Lord God is upon Me, Because the Lord has anointed Me To bring good news to the afflicted; He has sent Me to bind up the brokenhearted, To proclaim liberty to captives, And freedom to prisoners; To proclaim the favorable year of the Lord, And the day of vengeance of our God; To comfort all who mourn." Isaiah 61:1–2 (LSB)

That's the power of grace. It doesn't just forgive. It heals. It restores. It shapes us, and it turns weakness into strength and suffering into a testimony.

And it's available to you. Right now!

In the wreckage.

In the mess.

In the place where you think grace can't possibly reach.

It can. And it will. If you let it.

Chapter 14

The Spirit Received: When the Fire Ignites

The Church on Fire

"As for me, I baptize you with water for repentance, but He who is coming after me is mightier than I, and I am not fit to remove His sandals; He will baptize you with the Holy Spirit and fire." Matthew 3:11 (LSB)

John promised the fire would come after Jesus' ascension. Paul explained when that Spirit is received:

"Having also believed, you were sealed in Him with the Holy Spirit of promise." Ephesians 1:13 (LSB)

When I first started writing this chapter, it was titled "Baptism of Fire." I believed what many sincere Christians teach—that there *is* a second baptism, a distinct experience with the Holy Spirit that comes after salvation and water baptism.

I believed the disciples' experience at Pentecost was the pattern for every believer. I have been back and forth like so many others before me. This belief is one of the foundational reasons for this book.

But as I studied Scripture while writing, it felt like the Holy Spirit was correcting me. I began to see why the disciples had to wait for Pentecost because the Spirit had not yet been given to anyone (John 7:39). Jesus had to die, rise, ascend, and send the Helper. That was a one-time event in redemptive history, not a repeatable pattern. But there were

120 present at Pentecost. When did the disciples receive Holy Spirit?

When Did the Disciples Receive the Holy Spirit?

Before we go any further, I need to address something. For years, I believed I was missing something critical—a second baptism, the baptism of fire that would give me God's power. And if you've wrestled with feeling deficient or disconnected like I did, you're not alone. Because the debate around this has left a lot of good men feeling exactly that way.

First, we have my teaching growing up that speaking in tongues is no longer a gift or available from one side of the spectrum, and the opposite is that if you don't speak in tongues, you haven't been baptized by or in Holy Spirit. This creates a sense of, "Well, I guess I'm not good enough," or "Maybe the spiritual gifts don't exist as they say."

John 20:22 says that right after the resurrection, Jesus appeared to the disciples, breathed on them, and said, "Receive Holy Spirit."

But then in Acts 1, He tells them to wait in Jerusalem because they're about to receive the Holy Spirit at Pentecost.

So, which is it? Did they receive Him in John 20, or at Pentecost in Acts 2?

I had to wrestle with this myself because I'd been taught one thing, believed another for years, and neither one made complete sense when I laid it all out on the table. What I'm about to share is what I believe the Holy Spirit showed me while I was writing this book. You might believe something different—and that's okay. I'm not here to draw lines in the sand. I'm here to tell you what I see in Scripture and let the Holy Spirit do His work in you.

Here's what I believe is happening in John 20:22.

When Jesus breathed on them, the Greek word used is *enephusēsen*. That word appears only one other time in all of Scripture—Genesis 2:7, when God breathed life into Adam and man became a living being.

I don't think that's a coincidence. I believe Jesus was acting as the second Adam, breathing spiritual life into His disciples. This looks to me like their regeneration moment—when they were born again, when the Spirit came into them to make them new creations.

But why did the power not manifest? Why did they still have to wait for Pentecost?

Because what I see in Scripture is that being born again and being empowered for mission are connected but not identical. The Spirit came into them in John 20 to give them new life. The Spirit came upon them at Pentecost to empower them for what was coming next—the birth of the Church, the mission to the ends of the earth.

This wasn't two baptisms. What I believe happened was one massive transition that unfolded in stages for them because they lived in a unique moment in redemptive history. They were the bridge between the old covenant and the new. They were the first to experience what we now receive the moment we believe.

I believe their experience was transitional, not our pattern to repeat.

And here's where the Church has gotten itself tied in knots for centuries. Some said, "See? Two experiences! You get saved, then later you get the Spirit!" Others said, "No, it all happens at once!" And both camps dug in, built their denominations, wrote their statements of faith, and stopped talking to each other.

Meanwhile, the Holy Spirit—the Helper Jesus promised—got left out of the conversation entirely. We stopped teaching about Him because we couldn't agree on the timeline. We stopped expecting His power because we were too busy defending our position.

The devil doesn't care which ditch you fall in, as long as you're not walking on the road.

So, here's what I'm asking you to do: Don't take my word for it. Don't just accept what your denomination taught you, either. Go to Scripture yourself. Ask the Holy Spirit to show you. Because this isn't about winning a theological argument—it's about understanding when and how you received the Helper, so you can finally open the door and let Him function.

The Day of Pentecost:

After Pentecost, Scripture is clear: the Holy Spirit is given immediately when we believe (Ephesians 1:13). We don't wait for a second baptism.

The Spirit is sealed in us the moment we surrender to Christ. But many believers—like me—go years without knowing Him, without opening the door to let Him function.

That awakening is often so intense it's often called a 'baptism of fire'—I certainly thought it was. The experience can feel overwhelming and transformative, but it's not a separate baptism.

It's the first time we truly surrendered to the Helper we were promised but had never acknowledged.

Let's Talk About Water, Spirit, and Baptism

Before we go any further, we need to straighten out what people get tangled up about: **water, Spirit, and baptism.** Because if you don't understand what these words mean in Scripture, you'll spend your whole life confused about what you're missing.

Three different things. Not the same:

1. **Born of Water and Spirit (John 3:5-7)**

"Jesus answered, 'Truly, truly, I say to you, unless one is born of water and the Spirit, he cannot enter the kingdom of God. That which is born of the flesh is flesh, and that which is born of the Spirit is spirit.'" John 3:5-6 (LSB)

The “water” here is NOT baptism. It’s a **natural birth**—being born physically. Jesus is talking to Nicodemus about two births:

Born of water = **flesh** (your physical birth from your mother’s womb)

Born of Spirit = **spiritual rebirth** (becoming alive in Christ)

You were born once in the flesh. You must be born again in the Spirit. Two births. Not two baptisms.

2. **Baptism in Water (Public Declaration)**

Baptism isn't a box you check on your church membership card. It's not about getting wet in front of your family so they can take pictures. In God's eyes, baptism is a burial. Water baptism is the outward sign—a public declaration of the death and resurrection you’ve chosen to follow. You go under the water dead, identifying with Christ’s death and burial. You come up alive, raised with Him in newness of life.

It’s not magic. It doesn’t save you. It’s the picture of what’s already happening inside you.

3. **The Holy Spirit—Given at Belief**

“In Him, you also, after listening to the message of truth, the gospel of your salvation—having also believed, you were sealed in Him with the Holy Spirit of promise.” Ephesians 1:13 (LSB)

This is where most believers miss it. **The moment you truly believe, the Holy Spirit is given to you.** Not at baptism. Not at a second experience. At belief. He's present. He's sealed in you. He's available.

But here's the problem: like me, many believers go their entire lives without ever opening the door to let Him function.

Have you opened the door to the greatest promised gift we will ever know?

One Baptism, But Most Believers Only Experience Half

Paul says it clearly: *"One Lord, one faith, one baptism"* (Ephesians 4:5).

There is ONE baptism—the complete package of water (outward declaration) and Spirit (inward power). But here's what happens to most believers:

They believe → **The Holy Spirit is given** (Ephesians 1:13)

They get baptized in water → **Public declaration made.**

But they never open the door → **The Spirit is present but not functioning.**

Why? Because they don't know about Him. They were never taught about the Helper. No one told them there was a Guide, a Teacher, a Comforter waiting to lead them into all truth. We've never experienced Holy Spirit or recognized His voice.

So, when people ask, "Are there two baptisms?" what they're really asking is: "Why did I get baptized in water but never experience the fire? Why do I feel like something's missing?"

The answer: You didn't experience two separate baptisms. **You experienced half of one baptism.**

You got the water—the public statement. But you never invited the Spirit to function. You never opened the door. You never gave Him access to purify, empower, guide, and ignite you from the inside out.

The Fire Isn't a Second Baptism—It's Opening the Door

Once I opened that door at nineteen, I was on fire. I thought anything and everything was possible. I wanted it to be that "baptism of fire" I had heard about. In reality, it was simply the moment I finally invited the Holy Spirit to do what He came to do—to guide me, teach me, empower me, and consume me. It was the moment I realized I wasn't alone and could not do it on my own.

Jesus delivers the promise based on belief. But giving Him access depends on when we open the door and let Him in.

Before we go too far into this, let me ask: How can you open the door to someone you don't know exists?

I stood there giving my life to Jesus at the age of nine. The Holy Spirit was given to me that day, sealed in me according to Ephesians 1:13, but I never knew about Him. I never heard His name. I didn't know how to listen for His voice. I never knew a Helper was waiting to guide me. For nearly ten years, I carried the Holy Spirit inside me, but I had never let Him function because I didn't know about Him.

The Promise Fulfilled

The disciples had already believed in Jesus, walked with Him, watched Him die, and saw Him rise again. But something still hadn't happened. They were waiting on a promise.

Then it came:

"When the day of Pentecost had come, they were all together in one place. And suddenly a noise like a violent rushing wind came from heaven, and it filled the whole house where they were sitting. And tongues that looked like fire appeared to them, distributing themselves, and a tongue rested on each one of them. And they were all filled with the Holy Spirit and began to speak with different tongues, as the Spirit was giving them the ability to speak out." Acts 2:1-4 (LSB)

That was the fire. That was the moment the Spirit—who had been with them—now came to fully dwell IN them and empower them. The church didn't begin at the altar; it wasn't even built yet. It started with fire.

Peter confirmed it clearly: *"Repent, and each of you be baptized in the name of Jesus Christ for the forgiveness of your sins, and you will receive the gift of the Holy Spirit." Acts 2:38 (LSB)*

And Paul echoes it in Ephesians 4:5: "One Lord, one faith, one baptism."

There is one baptism—water and Spirit together. But let's be clear about when the Spirit comes:

The Holy Spirit is given at belief (Ephesians 1:13). The moment you truly believe, you are sealed with the Spirit. But being sealed with the Spirit and opening your life to His function are two different things.

Think of it like this: Jesus stands at the door and knocks (Revelation 3:20). When you believe, the Spirit takes up residence. But many believers never open the door fully. They never invite Him to guide their steps, speak into their decisions, empower their witness, or purify their hearts.

The "fire" isn't a second baptism. It's what happens when you finally give the Spirit access to function in your life.

Some of us encounter these awakening moments after we believe. Others—like me—don't meet Him until years later. Not because He wasn't there, but because we didn't know to look for Him.

I Asked Holy Spirit to Come, Now How Do I Get It?

If the Spirit is given at belief, why don't I feel Him? Why isn't He functioning in my life? That's the question I wrestled with for ten years.

We make this more complicated than it is. God isn't hiding His Spirit from you. You were sealed with the Spirit the moment you believed (Ephesians 1:13). But God also doesn't force His way into your daily life. He stands at the door and knocks (Revelation 3:20). He waits for you to open it.

"So if you, being evil, know how to give good gifts to your children, how much more will your heavenly Father give the Holy Spirit to those who ask Him?" Luke 11:13 (LSB)

Notice the word "ask." The Spirit is already given. But you have to invite Him to function.

Ten years after I believed and was baptized, I finally met Holy Spirit on a Sunday morning in Colorado Springs, Colorado.

I had been told I had time to grow, time to prepare, maybe even time to become a pastor one day. But I misunderstood. I thought that meant I had time to drift, time to figure it out later. I didn't realize what I was missing. I just didn't get it then. The relationship.

It was a Sunday morning in the barracks at Fort Carson, Colorado. I had the television on and was getting my wall locker ready for inspection the next day. I had this thought, "You need to go to church." I asked myself, "What?" Again, my thoughts said, "Go to church." I'm game, so I replied, "I don't know where any churches are!" About that time, a commercial came on the television for a local church in Colorado Springs. "Hmm, maybe I should go," is the next thought that pops into my mind.

I found myself driving around town looking for some stupid church mumbling under my breath, thinking I was stupid or crazy, one of the two.

After about my 5th turn around the area, I thought the church was supposed to be as I rolled up the stop light, I told God, "I'm going back to the barracks, I'm done looking." I turned, and guess what was right in front of me? That church. Yes, I parked and headed towards the door.

An elderly gentleman met me at the front door, pointed me to the sanctuary door, where another man was holding that door. "Man, these folks are fancy!" As I entered the sanctuary door, a rush of air hit me in the face. I didn't think anything of it at first, like maybe it was just the air conditioning and the opening of the door. "But the door was being held open."

But now I felt something, fear? Guilt? It was overwhelming, whatever it was. I began looking for a seat, and they were all full, and I didn't know a soul. "Should I leave?" Before I could turn around, there was another man, an usher maybe, who led me to the front row on the left side of the sanctuary. "Oh, Great! Front row seat."

That was the last thing I remember before my heart nearly exploded, and from what I had no idea. It didn't feel like fear, though I was afraid. It didn't feel like shame or guilt but instead was affecting me physically. I never heard a note of music or a word of the sermon. I cried sitting in the front row the entire time. I didn't even know why.

After the sermon, the invitation, and the closing, there I sat. Just then able to slightly compose myself. The world around me was silent, and I felt just a little bit scared and confused.

A man, the pastor, was standing before me when I looked up. As we spoke, he asked me if I had ever asked Jesus into my life. My answer was yes. He then asked if I had ever experienced or met the Holy Spirit. That answer was no.

That pastor invited me to his home and introduced me to other military soldiers and cadets. I was given the opportunity to join a class about spiritual gifts with the idea of learning about them and finding out which one or two God had gifted me with.

This was the beginning of a wild ride.

"And it is God who establishes us with you in Christ, and has anointed us, and who has also put his seal on us and given us his Spirit in our hearts as a guarantee."
2 Corinthians 1:21–22 (ESV)

A guarantee in our hearts, a seal on us, an anointing established by God.

What else do we need?

Chapter 15

Salvation Clarity—Born of the Spirit

Salvation Isn't Just Believing Jesus Exists.

We've explained earlier that belief in the Greek runs far deeper. It's not an emotional moment at the altar or a sentence you repeated because someone told you to. It's a rebirth, and that rebirth happens in the Spirit.

"Jesus answered, 'Truly, truly, I say to you, unless one is born of water and the Spirit, he cannot enter the kingdom of God. That which is born of the flesh is flesh, and that which is born of the Spirit is spirit. Do not marvel that I said to you, "You must be born again."' John 3:5–7 (LSB)

Jesus is talking about two births here: born of water (your natural birth in the flesh) and born of the Spirit (your spiritual rebirth). You were born once physically. You must be born again spiritually.

The Holy Spirit is given to you the moment you believe; you are sealed with Him (Ephesians 1:13). But being sealed with the Spirit and opening your life to His function are two different things.

But here's the question most believers never ask themselves:

The Spirit was given at belief. But have I given Him access? Have I invited Him to function in my life?

A lot of us try to live in Spirit power we've never accessed because we've never opened the door. This isn't about condemnation, it's about clarity.

Ask yourself honestly:

Not:
"Do I attend church?"
"Did I get baptized?"
"Do I help with the Youth?"

But:
"Have I opened the door to the Helper?"
"Have I invited the Spirit to guide, teach, empower, and purify me?"
"Is the fire burning, or is the Spirit still standing outside, knocking?"

If the answer is no, it doesn't mean God has rejected you. He didn't forget about you or deemed you undeserving. It means He's still inviting you to open the door.

Do you feel adopted into the family of God?

"For you have not received a spirit of slavery leading to fear again, but you have received a spirit of adoption as sons by which we cry out, 'Abba! Father!'"
Romans 8:15 (LSB)

The Door Opens

That day in Colorado Springs wasn't a second baptism. It wasn't me "getting" the Holy Spirit for the first time.

According to Ephesians 1:13, He was sealed in me the moment I believed at age nine.

But it was the first time I opened the door.

For ten years, the Holy Spirit had been with me—present, waiting, available. But I never knew His name. I never knew to invite Him in. I never gave Him access to guide my steps, speak into my life, or ignite the fire I was called to carry.

That Sunday morning, I finally met the Helper. And when I opened the door, the fire ignited.

This is what John the Baptist was pointing to when he said, "He will baptize you with the Holy Spirit and fire" (Matthew 3:11). Not two baptisms—one baptism—water and Spirit. But the fire doesn't ignite until you open the door. The gift was given, I received it, but I never opened the package.

Paul asked the Ephesian believers: *"Did you receive the Holy Spirit when you believed?" (Acts 19:2)*

The question isn't, "Did God give you the Spirit?" He did—at surrender, if you surrendered.

The question is: "Did you receive Him? Did you open the door? Did you give Him access to function in your life?"

Did you even know or hear about the greatest gift known to mankind that wanted to come and dwell inside of you?

Many believers can't answer yes.

What the Fire Does

The baptism of the Holy Spirit isn't an experience you will ever forget. The fire of God *does something* in you. It changes you from the inside out. Your mind, body, soul, heart, and spirit go through a refining fire, empowering you, guiding, and connecting you to the rest of the body of Christ.

Purifies

"But who can endure the day of His coming? And who can stand when He appears? For He is like a refiner's fire and like a launderer's soap. And He will sit as a smelter and purifier of silver. He will purify the sons of Levi and refine them like gold and silver, so that they may present to the Lord offerings in righteousness." Malachi 3:2–3 (ESV)

Empowers

"But you will receive power when the Holy Spirit has come upon you; and you shall be My witnesses both in Jerusalem, and in all Judea and Samaria, and even to the remotest part of the earth." Acts 1:8 (LSB)

Guides

"Your ears will hear a word behind you, saying, 'This is the way, walk in it,' whenever you turn to the right or to the left." Isaiah 30:21 (LSB)

Unites

"And He gave some as apostles, some as prophets, some as evangelists, some as pastors and teachers, for the

equipping of the saints for the work of ministry, for the building up of the body of Christ; until we all attain to the unity of the faith, and of the knowledge of the Son of God, to a mature man, to the measure of the stature which belongs to the fullness of Christ."
Ephesians 4:11–13 (NASB 1995)

At fifteen, one of my daughters was diagnosed with severe aplastic anemia. The result would lead to many procedures and finally a long stay in a children's hospital for a bone marrow transplant. But her story is about the fire of the Holy Spirit.

She wasn't able to attend high school due to having no immune system. It was unsafe. But when she was asked to go to the IHOP (not the pancake place, the International House of Prayer) in Kansas City, Missouri, we allowed her to go. None of her friends knew what was wrong with her. She wasn't even able to attend church very often, either. It seemed like she should go.

I remember her phone call on the way home. One of excitement, joy, and an unbelievable story. All I know is the sermon was on how God has used fire. To communicate in a bush, to destroy, to refine, to guide, to consume, to cleanse, and in judgment.

At the end, one of the leaders asked if anyone needed healing to raise their hand. My understanding is that after some prodding, my daughter raised her hand. A lady she didn't know, and still does not to this day, prayed for her and put her hands on her shoulders. My daughter told me she felt so hot inside that she broke out in a sweat and thought she might stink.

When this mystery lady was done praying, she whispered, "Honey, I don't know what's wrong with you, but God said he just healed your blood." How could she have known anything? Not to mention the sensation of being so hot in her body that she sweats.

Was she healed? The doctors still had their say, and we still had a journey ahead of us, but I'll tell you this: something happened in that moment. Whether it was the start of a process or the completion of one, the fire of God touched her. And when His fire touches you, you are never the same.

"Then one of the seraphim flew to me with a burning coal in his hand, which he had taken from the altar with tongs. He touched my mouth with it and said, 'Behold, this has touched your lips; and your guilt is taken away and atonement is made for your sin.'" Isaiah 6:6–7

If God's fire can speak from a bush, lead His people by night, consume a water-soaked offering with fire, cleanse a prophet's lips, and heal a young girl's blood, what can it do in you?

Don't just study the fire. Don't just hear about it. Ask for it. Wait for it. Let it touch you.

Father, I don't just want to hear stories about Your fire; I want to be consumed by it, cleansed by it, purified, guided by it, and burning inside. Throw away the chaff that keeps me from You. Purify my heart, empower my hands, guide my steps, and unite me with Your people. Help me to live in you and You in me. Let my life and my purpose burn for You. In the name above *All* names, Jesus, Jesus, Jesus. I pray. Amen.

So, what now? We don't need another slogan. We don't need another conference to pump us up for the weekend. We don't need another revival. We need a return to *relationship*. To the One who is calling us home.

Every revival, every move of God, starts with one surrendered heart. If the fire is going out in us, no wonder it's gone out in the Church.

Chapter 16

When Programs Replace Power

From Spirit-Led to Program-Driven

God's Church

When you think of the word "Church," what do you see? A building and a parking lot? God's Church is not a business or a building where people gather to worship. We are the Church. You are the Church.

You! With your story, your scars, your faith, and your fire. If you burn, we burn. If you grow cold, we grow cold. If you walk Spirit-led, we walk Spirit-led.

"Or do you not know that your body is a temple of the Holy Spirit within you, whom you have from God, and that you are not your own? For you have been bought for a price; therefore glorify God in your body."
1 Corinthians 6:19–20 (LSB)

We've been taught growing up to look at Church like it's somewhere we go to find God. When the whole time God has been looking at us, because "we" are where He desires to go. We are a temple where God exists in this place.

Does this change how you walk into a Sunday morning or any other day, or when you commune with our creator?

If His Church is made of His people, then how we move together is just as important as who we are.

Why So Many Buildings Are Empty of Power

"These people honor Me with their lips, but their heart is far from Me. And in vain do they worship Me, teaching as doctrines the commandments of men."
Matthew 15:8-9 (LSB)

So, what happened? How did we go from Acts 2, where the presence of God was so real that thousands were saved in a single day, to buildings full of people who barely expect God to show up?
It didn't happen overnight. And it wasn't one person's fault. It was a slow drift, a slight deviation that, over generations, led us miles from where we started.

Here's the truth most people don't want to say out loud: Many pastors were trained in knowledge, not anointing. They went to seminary and learned theology, church history, Greek, and Hebrew.

- They learned how to structure a sermon in three points and how to manage a budget.
- They learned about God and who He is, but not who they are.

But were they taught how to WAIT on God?

How to hear His voice?

How to host His presence. How to move when the Spirit moves, even if it wrecks the schedule.

They inherited a system, not a fire.

And here's the part that's hard to hear:
You can't give what you don't carry.
If a pastor has never been undone in the presence of God, how can he lead others there? If he's never seen Holy Spirit move in power, why would he make room for it in the service?

If his training taught him to stay in control, why would he surrender control to the Spirit? This isn't an attack. It's an explanation.

The System Failed Them Before it Failed You

But here's where responsibility comes in: Just because they inherited a broken system doesn't mean they're not responsible for what they pass on. And just because your pastor can't lead you into the fire doesn't mean you have to stay in the cold.

The generation rising up right now—Gen Z, Gen Alpha—they're not like the generations before them. They fact-check everything. They can smell fake a mile away.

They've seen enough performance, enough polish, and enough empty words.
What they're hungry for is REAL. Not some social media experience.

And if the church can't give them the reality of God — His presence, His power, His transformation — they'll walk.

Not because they don't want Jesus. But because they refuse to settle for a version of Christianity that looks nothing like what they read in the Book of Acts.

So, the question isn't just "What's wrong with the church?" The question is: "What are YOU going to do about it?"

The Drift Begins—One Half Turn from True North

Drift didn't start with rebellion. It began with tiny shifts, disagreements, personal preferences, and traditions, just one half a degree at a time.

The Church doesn't notice it at first. The worship music has changed. The teaching still quotes Scripture, but no longer teaches us to avoid sin, but to just ask for forgiveness.

The faces are still familiar. But somewhere along the way, the relationship gave way to routine, convenience, to compromise, and the fire gave way to the world.

The healing touch of the Father isn't received, and the scars and wounds from our past still haunt us. We never see ourselves as having our debt already paid. Never trust what we can't know unless we see it.

The enemy has groomed the world to believe true north is the opposite direction.

A Church's surrender will never go deeper than its People's surrender.

When the people choose comfort over calling, and compromise over truth, the Church will too. When the people walk out of alignment with God, the whole body eventually ends up miles from where the Spirit was leading.

In many cases, division comes—and when another group is formed, they often start even further from the Spirit than where they began. Another Church is now divided.

"Now I urge you, brothers and sisters, by the name of our Lord Jesus Christ, that you all agree and that there be no divisions among you, but that you be made complete in the same mind and in the same judgment."
1 Corinthians 1:10 (LSB)

Have we forgotten from whence we came? Have we forgotten we are all one in the body of Christ? One God, one creator, one family. Yet we believed in the world's opinion and looked at each other as the enemy.

We've judged each other as evil and unforgiving, morally bankrupt, and a liar. We've made ourselves gods. Not very loving ones either.

There used to be a movement and even a movie, "WWJD" (What Would Jesus Do?) But like so many movements and revivals, they come and go just as easily as the feel-good moments they created. "Now I urge you, brothers and sisters, by the name of our Lord Jesus . . . " How far we have come, in the wrong direction.

"Therefore, I, the prisoner of the Lord, urge you to walk in a manner worthy of the calling with which you have been called, with all humility and gentleness, with patience, bearing with one another in love, being diligent to keep the unity of the Spirit in the bond of peace. There is one body and one Spirit, just as you also were called in one hope of your calling; one Lord, one faith, one baptism, one God and Father of all who is over all and through all and in all." Ephesians 4:1-6 (LSB)

A spark is useless unless it catches . . . And the only fuel it needs is your surrender. We need a spark to light our fires. We need to bear with one another in love, not judgment and hate.

Every revival, every move of God, starts with one surrendered heart. And if the fire has gone out in the Church, it's because the fire is going out in us.

Why Programs Feel Safer

So why do Churches drift toward programs instead of power?

Because programs are manageable, you can measure them. You can track attendance, count baptisms, and monitor engagement. You know what's coming. You can plan for it. Budget for it. Staff it. Market it.
Programs give leadership control. And control feels responsible. It feels wise. It feels like good stewardship.

But here's the trap: programs produce attendees, not disciples. They create crowds, not carriers of fire. They build organizations, but they don't build the Church.

The Spirit, on the other hand, is unpredictable. You can't put God on a timeline. You can't measure the movement of the Holy Spirit with metrics. You can't control who He touches or when He shows up or how long He stays.

And that terrifies leadership that's been trained to manage outcomes.

So, we make a trade. We trade the risk of following the Spirit for the safety of running a program. We trade the unknown for the predictable. We trade power for control.

And we convince ourselves it is wisdom.

We tell ourselves we're being responsible. We honor people's time. We're excellent. We're reaching more people by being organized.

But somewhere in that trade, we lost what made us the Church in the first place.

Because you can build a big crowd with programs, but only the Spirit builds the bride.

You can create a great event. But only the Spirit creates transformation.

You can fill a building. But only the Spirit fills a life.

And here's the cost nobody talks about when you choose programs over power, you train people to expect less. You teach them that church is something you attend, not something you are. You model that faith is predictable, safe, and containable.

And then we wonder why the next generation walks away the moment life gets hard.
Because we gave them a program when they needed power.

The question isn't whether your Church runs programs.

The question is: who's in charge?

Because when programs replace power, we lose more than anointing.

We lose the next generation. We lose transformation. We lose the very thing that makes us the Church.

And the only way back isn't another strategy.

It's surrender.

Chapter 17

The Church's Fear and the Spirit's Fire

When the Church Lost Its Flame

When did we trade the fire for fog machines? When did Altar calls, praying for and laying hands on those in need, become optional, and Holy Spirit become . . . polite?

"Is anyone among you sick? Let him call for the elders of the church, and let them pray over him, anointing him with oil in the name of the Lord. And the prayer of faith will save the one who is sick, and the Lord will raise him up. And if he has committed sins, he will be forgiven."
James 5:14–15 (ESV)

Nobody woke up one day and said, "Let's ignore the Spirit." But little by little, we got tired of the mess. We watched pastors and evangelists like Oral Roberts and Kathryn Kuhlman praying and sharing the gospel. Then we watched as they began healing those afflicted on live television. Those that disagreed or no longer believe in miracles began to murmur that they thought it was for show. But was it?

We became tired of the unpredictability. Tired of the questions we couldn't get answers to. We stopped believing God might actually heal all those people. It made us look bad; they started calling people names like Christian Holy

Rollers. The very aspect of that being true was appalling to some.

Again, Satan smiled.

It was easier to ignore it than it was to defend these things. After all that didn't happen in our church, on my block, in my city. Why not?

So, we made our Church and worship manageable, comfortable, more of a living room than a hospital. Somewhere safe. And in doing so, we stopped inviting the flame.

Ironically, we became the show. Not all miracles or healings were on TV, but when we called them fake, they stopped happening everywhere, including in our own Churches.

Have you ever had a heart attack in the desert in 125-degree weather and 90 minutes from the closest hospital and walked out of the hospital with no heart damage? Seven aspirin may have saved my life, the 3 nitroglycerine pills didn't touch the pain, nor the three shots of morphine.

It wasn't until they opened the vein and placed three stents in my Left Anterior Descending artery (LAD) that the pain finally stopped.

What happened next defied every medical expectation. The doctors told me that only about twelve percent of people in my condition survive, and even fewer without permanent heart damage. But I did.

My heart showed no signs of trauma. No scar tissue. No loss of function. I shouldn't have walked out of that hospital; I shouldn't have even made it to the hospital, but I did, and I walked out whole.

You can call that luck if you want, but I know better. That was the hand of God reaching into a hopeless situation and rewriting the outcome. It wasn't just a physical rescue; it was a divine reminder that my life wasn't over and that my purpose was far from complete.

Every beat of my heart since that day is a testimony that grace doesn't just forgive. Sometimes, it sustains, restores, and gives you a second chance to walk out what you were always meant to do.

When did we start creating experiences instead of contending for presence?

We wanted sermons that inspired, but not a Spirit that interrupts. We stopped laying hands. Stopped lingering. Stopped listening. We treated communion with our Lord like a habit instead of the remembrance of sacrifice. And now our sons and daughters don't know what it means to be undone in the presence of God.

"I know your works: you are neither cold nor hot. Would that you were either cold or hot! So, because you are lukewarm, and neither hot nor cold, I will spit you out of my mouth." Revelation 3:15–16 (ESV)

We can build buildings. We can host conferences. We can teach theology.

But without fire, without discipleship, we're just stacking wood that never burns. The early Church didn't grow because it had great planning. It grew because the presence of God disrupted everything. They let God's plan prevail, not their own. It started with tongues of fire. And somewhere along the way, those who didn't receive it made excuses so it would go away.

"Having the appearance of godliness, but denying its power. Avoid such people."
2 Timothy 3:5 (ESV)

We didn't lose Holy Spirit's presence. He was grieved. *We exchanged the fire for quiet control.* The sanctuary stayed full for a while, but the altar became empty.

Bringing Order to The Storm

This is a beckoning call to the Church Jesus created. This is the trumpet blast to wake her up. And some folks won't like that. Especially the ones who built their lives and ministries around keeping the fire contained, but the seats filled. All the while keeping the flock comfortable, unoffended, and unrealistically safe.

Jesus stood in the gap for you and is *still* standing there. He's trying to replace what was stolen, but we won't let Him. This is the time to shake the bride awake before the groom shows up.

"And He saw that there was no one, And was astonished that there was no one to intercede; Then His own arm brought salvation to Him, And His righteousness upheld Him." Isaiah 59:16 (LSB)

Before full surrender comes, we must confront the modern Church's fear of the supernatural move of the Holy Spirit. We must expose how control, comfort, and counterfeit spirits have quenched the fire God meant for His people.

We sit and watch pastors calling for those who need prayer, but no one comes. Why? Is it shame, embarrassment? Have we become like judges so much that our own local body isn't trusted to pray for us?

Until pastors begin to call out to those who are sick, to those who are struggling financially, looking for a job, dying of disease, suffering from depression, about to lose their marriage, no one will come to the front for prayer.

The body will continue to suffer in silence without surrendering because of our self-image.

This very moment is a call out, not of shame or accusation, but of repentance and reawakening, of return for the prodigal Church. For the children of God to walk in surrendered power, not polished performance. And not because it's mean. Not because it's reckless. But because God's truth must burn where people have gotten comfortable living in smoke.

Playing It Safe: The Moments We Can't Explain

Was it safe for Jesus to flip tables in the temple? Were there feelings of comfort when Elijah called down fire in front of a nation? Let's not forget when John the Baptist wore camel hair and told religious leaders they were snakes.

Yet Peter preached the first Spirit-filled sermon to the same people who had just crucified Jesus. So scripturally speaking, we're in good company.

What is stirring up isn't a rebellion. It's way beyond a revival. It's a return. We're not just drawing a line, but we also offer a hand and a prayer.

Just as Jesus speaks to the Churches in Revelation, He's not just saying "You are off track"; Jesus is saying, "There's a better way, and it's through fire, not fear."

"For the time will come when they will not tolerate sound doctrine, but wanting to have their ears tickled, they will accumulate for themselves teachers in accordance with their own desires, and they will turn their ears away from the truth and will turn aside to myths. But as for you, use self-restraint in all things, endure hardship, do the work of an evangelist, fulfill your ministry."
2 Timothy 4:3–5 (NASB 1995)

God's Church doesn't need better programs. More small groups and Bible study classes. She needs her fire back. Not the fire we can control with lighting cues and schedules, but the fire that disrupts, transforms, and makes us uncomfortable enough to actually surrender.

Just because you've never experienced something doesn't mean it doesn't exist in others. The absence of fire in your experience doesn’t mean the flame has gone out; it just means we’ve learned to live without it.

That fire is still available. It’s still as fierce and holy as it was in the upper room, still able to shake the ground and change hearts in an instant. But it doesn’t come cheaply.

It requires that we stop playing it safe and start playing for keeps. That we trade comfort for Holy Spirit’s presence. That we give up our control for His leading. That we let go of our preferred way of doing things, safe way, and our predictable services and prepackaged faith, for His *unpredictable* power.

The question isn't whether God still moves. The question is whether we're willing to let Him.

“Therefore, since we receive a kingdom which cannot be shaken, let us show gratitude, by which we may offer to God an acceptable service with reverence and awe; for our God is a consuming fire.” Hebrews 12:28–29 (NASB 1995)

Prayer:

Father, set my heart on fire again. Burn away my love of comfort, my need for control, and anything that keeps me from fully following You. Teach me to trade safety for surrender and predictability for Your presence. Let Your consuming fire refines me from the inside out, until every part of my life reflects Your power, Your truth, and Your glory. In Jesus Holy name, Amen.

Chapter 18

Fear . . . Not From God

Fear is one of the enemy's oldest weapons. Not the healthy fear of God that brings wisdom, but the paralyzing fear that keeps us silent, passive, and powerless. The kind of fear that makes us choose safety over surrender. And nowhere has this fear taken deeper root than in the Western Church, where we've traded the supernatural for the manageable, the Spirit's fire for institutional comfort.

What Are We Afraid Of?

What are we afraid of? I'm serious. If you stop and think about how the Church in Western civilization has changed. From healing the sick, making the deaf hear, the lame walk, and the dead rise, to colored lights, fog machines, a few laying on of hands, and little to no prophecy being spoken during worship.

"Truly, truly I say to you, the one who believes in Me, the works that I do, he will do also; and greater works than these he will do, because I am going to the Father."
John 14:12 (LSB)

Men fear what they can't control. Men fear what they don't understand. And nothing breaks our control and goes beyond our understanding like the fire of the Holy Spirit.

Fear doesn’t come in a frontal attack. It drains the courage out of men one whisper at a time. It redefines spiritual leadership through oppression and a false sense of self-worth.

“Be of sober spirit, be on the alert. Your adversary, the devil, prowls around like a roaring lion, seeking someone to devour.” 1 Peter 5:8 (NASB 1995)

The Spirit of Control and Compromise

There's a spirit at work in homes and Churches that doesn't announce itself. It doesn't wave a flag or demand attention. It operates through exhaustion, through unresolved pain, through leadership that's afraid to confront. This spirit of control and manipulation doesn't need to yell, it whispers.

It whispers: *"Stay quiet. Don't push back. Keep the peace. Don't ruffle feathers. Let someone else fight."*

This isn't about gender; this spirit operates wherever there's a hunger for control paired with fear of confrontation. It thrives in complacency. It undermines God's design not to dominate, but to protect and lead in love.

The saying "old habits die hard" is truer in the Church than ever before. Repeating leads to retreating into safety. Into comfort. Into complacency and is not only redundant but also denies the spirit. Moves of God aren't allowed because we just don't do things that way.

"Be dressed in readiness, and keep your lamps lit. You are also to be like people who are waiting for their master when he returns from the wedding feast, so that they may immediately open the door for him when he comes and knocks." Luke 12:35–36 (NASB 1995)

Safe Religion Is Spiritually Dangerous

The early Church was built on Jesus, not on schedules, but with the piercing of His body on a cross. It started in an upper room with prayer and was delivered by fire. There was no plan for "revival," just the delivery of the gospel of Jesus Christ. There was no building. No sound system. Just streets and sidewalks to proclaim the prophecy fulfilled.

"When the day of Pentecost had come, they were all together in one place. And suddenly a noise like a violent rushing wind came from heaven, and it filled the whole house where they were sitting. And tongues that looked like fire appeared to them, distributing themselves, and a tongue rested on each one of them. And they were all filled with the Holy Spirit and began to speak with different tongues, as the Spirit was giving them the ability to speak out." Acts 2:1–4 (NASB 1995)

That doesn't sound very safe to me. Does it sound very safe to you?

What happens when we suppress the supernatural? What happens if their fear overcomes them and they don't see any tongues that look like fire? What happens when sermons replace surrender? Programming replaces presence. Men begin to feel disconnected, disillusioned, and dormant.

Men are hunter-gatherers, made to hunt, made like Adam to protect and guard the garden. Protect their families. Protect the flock.

Without the spirit of a warrior in the Church, there are no prayer warriors. No David. No Samson. Only Goliaths. Without Elijah, the Word goes unheard. Unexplained. Unbelieved. In homes and in Churches.

What's missing in most Churches today?

The fear of God, instead of the fear of man.

We weren't called to sit by and turn the other cheek, following along with culture. We were commanded to take ground, spreading the gospel to the ends of the earth. Fear of the unknown and difference of opinion was never supposed to be the thermostat of the Church. God has never whispered comfort, but He has commanded courage.

"Have I not commanded you? Be strong and courageous! Do not be terrified nor dismayed, for the Lord your God is with you wherever you go." Joshua 1:9 (NASB 1995)

Men Called to Courage

"Then the Lord God took the man and put him in the Garden of Eden to cultivate it and tend it." Genesis 2:15 (NASB 1995)

The battle for godly masculinity isn't new, but it's never been more urgent.

The enemy doesn't need to destroy men to dismantle families and Churches. He just needs them to do nothing. Convince them to step back. Stay quiet. Avoid conflict. Go with the flow. Trade boldness for comfort and leadership for survival.

That's the strategy. It's never a direct frontal assault, but a slow erosion.

And the primary tool? Fear-based leadership. Not fear of God. But fear of people, of the flock. Fear of being labeled toxic, controlling, outdated, or unloving. Fear of offending the wrong crowd or simply doing it wrong, so we don't do it at all.

When a man no longer leads from his Spirit, he starts leading from fear.

Men stop fighting and start folding. They prefer peace in the home and compromise. They think they're being loving and gentle when they're actually being disarmed. He starts calling silence wisdom when it's really just self-preservation.

The world creates a tired man. A man who's more worried about being liked than being obedient. A man who doesn't see the battle or know he's in one. But for too long, all men have seen is slavery and servitude instead of our royal priesthood in the kingdom. This is where the tide needs to turn.

"But you are a chosen people, a royal priesthood, a holy nation, a people for God's own possession, so that you may proclaim the excellencies of Him who has called you out of darkness into His marvelous light." 1 Peter 2:9 (NIV)

Royal priesthood doesn't mean robes and titles. It means fire, sacrifice, and surrender. And most of us were never taught how to carry that.

This isn't about being lord over all or authoritarianism. This is about godly authority rooted in surrender. When men stop leading spiritually, homes grow spiritually cold.

Prayer becomes occasional. Worship becomes optional. Scripture becomes silent.

And the worst part? The next generation thinks that's normal. Our culture has not only confused masculinity, but it's attempted to erase it altogether.

Young men grow up never seeing spiritual fathers. Never seeing men pray with authority, repent openly, worship freely. They've seen men achieve, succeed, and dominate, but rarely submit, lead in love, or walk humbly before God.

We have too many men in the Church who believe they're disqualified before they've even been discipled. But let's be clear: God is still calling men to stand up, speak out, and lead well.

While so many of us have been standing on the sidelines, God's been trying to send us in with the perfect play, not in perfection, but in presence, not in dominance, but in discernment, not in fear, but in faith.
You don't need a title. You don't need a platform. You don't need anyone's permission but God's.
You are called to lead your home. To speak the Word of God over your family. To war in prayer and worship. To break the cycles that try to own your name. To love your wife like Christ loves the Church. To train your children to stand in truth when the world celebrates lies.

This isn't about bravado, it's about surrender.

You're not called to be the loudest voice in the room or the first to speak. You're called to be the one who stays when others turn away. To be the one who loves when others walk away. To be the one who prays when no one else is watching.

"Be on the alert, stand firm in the faith, act like men, be strong." – 1 Corinthians 16:13 (LSB)

The strength you need isn't found in your past.
It's found in the Spirit of God who still speaks to *His* sons.

Chapter 19

The Personal Call

"Peter said to them, 'Repent, and each of you be baptized in the name of Jesus Christ for the forgiveness of your sins; and you will receive the gift of the Holy Spirit.'"
Acts 2:38 (LSB)

Like many who read the title of this book for the first time, maybe you, too, thought I was blaming my pastor or the Church. And I was, when confronted with the truth, and like every other human being, I pointed fingers elsewhere. But God didn't call them, He called ME! God won't hold them accountable for my surrender. He holds that for me.

Don't wait for revival weekends or someone else to bring the fire.

You are the starting point. Be baptized in water and fire. Live walking in the Spirit daily. Be the match that lights the fire and watch it spread.

"For this reason I remind you to kindle afresh the gift of God which is in you through the laying on of my hands. For God has not given us a spirit of timidity, but of power and love and discipline." 2 Timothy 1:6–7 (LSB)

But the fire God lights in you was never meant to stop with you. That's why it's meant to spread first to the people closest to you, then into the whole body, and then to every corner of the world.

The Corporate Church Ignition – When Your Fire Spreads

"You are the light of the world. A city set on a hill cannot be hidden; nor does anyone light a lamp and put it under a basket, but on the lampstand, and it gives light to all who are in the house. Let your light shine before men in such a way that they may see your good works, and glorify your Father who is in heaven." Matthew 5:14–16 (NASB 1995)

Our calling is more than gathering together to watch other people minister to God. When the Spirit is burning in you, prepare yourself to be that match that lights the fire. Holy Spirit will ignite those around you, not by force, but by overflow. Your obedience will ripple into your home, your small group, and your whole body.

The corporate Church is where we come together to worship, give thanks, and minister to God. But what Jesus created wasn't just a weekly meeting.

Not just a crowd, but people on assignment. Not just to worship God but to govern and exhort each other. Loving one another as Jesus commanded in John 13:34–35.

The first time Jesus mentioned His Church was when He told Simon Peter:

"I also say to you that you are Peter, and upon this rock I will build My church; and the gates of Hades will not overpower it." Matthew 16:18 (LSB)

The Church Jesus promised to build was, and still is, a body of believers called out from their homes, into the streets, into the world to carry His Kingdom into it. A people so rooted in Him that even hell itself can't break them apart. Meeting daily to break bread from house to house.

There were no massive Churches or places to gather. They moved from house to house, street to street, sharing the gospel of Jesus. All were children of God; all were called into the royal priesthood. But like anything free-flowing, man will think he needs to control it.

While the early Churches suffered from many of the same ailments we still suffer today, like envy, jealousy, traditions, and personal preference. The Apostle Paul talked and taught on many of these, not to shame the Church, but to keep her aligned with the Spirit's lead, free from man's control and full of God's power.

"But avoid foolish controversies and genealogies and strife and disputes about the Law, for they are useless and worthless. Reject a divisive person after a first and second warning, knowing that such a person has deviated from what is right and is sinning, being self-condemned."
Titus 3:9–11 (NASB 1995)

While we may have many witnesses, not all will testify. We each have our role, and more often than not, it is to serve instead of lead. The opposite of division is not control; it's humility. And humility always serves before it leads.

"But the greatest of you shall be your servant." Matthew 23:11 (NASB 1995)

And that's the question only you can answer, not for your Church, not for your pastor, but for yourself:

If the Holy Spirit in you can and will change everything, will you allow Him to change you first?

Staying Anchored to the Rock – An Enduring Flame

When the Spirit's fire burns in you, it's not shaken by the winds of culture or the waves of drift. It's steady because it's built on a Rock that cannot be moved.

This fire isn't meant to be a flash in the pan or a weekend fanning of the flame. It's given to burn steadily through the calm and through the storm because it's fixed to something immovable. That Rock is Christ. Your surrender to Him keeps the flame from blowing out when the wind changes. It lights the way in the storm. And no flood can douse it.

"For no one can lay a foundation other than the one which is laid, which is Jesus Christ." 1 Corinthians 3:11 (LSB)

If your life is anchored to Him, your fire will not just survive, it will create embers that run deep and spread. The Church's strength isn't in her size or structure, but in her foundation. Spirit-filled, surrendered lives form a body that stands, a cord that cannot be broken, a true band of brothers and sisters. Even when everything else in the world around you falls or fails.

"And if one can overpower him who is alone, two can resist him. A cord of three strands is not quickly torn apart." Ecclesiastes 4:12 (NASB 1995)

The Holy Spirit doesn't just set you ablaze; He plants your feet on something unshakable, immovable, and uncompromising, so your fire will outlast every storm.

"He alone is my rock and my salvation, my refuge; I will not be shaken." Psalm 62:6 (NASB 1995)

What do you see now, in this moment? Who do you hear?

Where is your fire, fully ablaze or on the verge of being snuffed out?

Chapter 20

When the Church Can't Give You What Jesus Promised

What You're Walking Into

"Not everyone who says to Me, 'Lord, Lord,' will enter the kingdom of heaven, but the one who does the will of My Father who is in heaven." Matthew 7:21 (LSB)

You got saved. Maybe in a living room, maybe in a church building, maybe alone in your car. But the moment was real. The conviction was real. Jesus became real to you. And then someone told you, "Now you need to find a Church." So, you did.

You walked through the doors expecting to find what you'd just experienced—that raw, undeniable presence of God. You were hungry. You were ready. You thought, "This is where I'll learn. This is where I'll grow. This is where I'll see the power of God I just read about in Acts."

But instead, you found . . . a show. Lights. Fog machines. A band that sounds like a concert. A sermon that feels like a TED Talk. Coffee. Comfortable seats and smiling faces. But no fire.

No healing. No deliverance. No transformation is happening in front of your eyes. No one falling on their face before God. No one is weeping at an altar. No sense that anything supernatural is even expected to happen.

It looks like, it feels like, just . . . performance. And you think: *"Is this it? Is this what Jesus died for?"*

Brother, sister, what you're sensing isn't doubt. It's discernment. Something *IS* missing. And it's not you.

The Word That Got Lost

"I also say to you that you are Peter, and upon this rock I will build My church; and the gates of Hades will not overpower it." Matthew 16:18 (LSB)

Here's something most people don't know: Jesus never used the word "Church" the way we use it today. He used a Greek word: *Ekklesia.*

And it didn't mean a building. It didn't mean Sunday service. It didn't mean an organization with a board, a budget, and a brand.

Ekklesia means *"the called-out ones."*

In ancient Greece, when the city leaders needed to make important decisions or take action, they would send a herald through the streets calling people out of their homes. These weren't just random crowds—these were citizens summoned with a purpose and called out. Assembled. On mission.

That's what Jesus meant. Not a place you GO to once a week. But a people you ARE every single day. The Church was never meant to be a building you enter. It was meant to be a body you belong to a living, breathing, movement of people carrying the presence of God into every corner of the world.

Acts 2:46-47 shows us what this looked like:

"Day by day continuing with one mind in the temple, and breaking bread from house to house, they were taking their meals together with gladness and sincerity of heart, praising God and having favor with all the people. And the Lord was adding to their number day by day those who were being saved." Acts 2:46–47 (NASB 1995)

They didn't meet once a week for 90 minutes and call it good. They lived it. Daily. House to house. Breaking bread together, praying for each other, and sharing their lives. And the Lord was adding to their number, not because they had a great marketing strategy, but because the presence of God was undeniable.

That's Ekklesia!

And somewhere along the way, we traded it for buildings, programs, and performances. The word "Church" today is overused and undervalued. It conjures images of parking lots, stained glass, and rows of people listening while someone talks at you.

It's become a place you attend, not a people, a kingdom you belong to.

But when I think of the Ekklesia? That word still burns with what Jesus intended. It should be like heaven where the angels sing, and every knee shall bow, and everyone is healed before the Lord!

The question is: Are you willing to pursue it even if the building you walked into doesn't?

You're probably asking: "But why? Why doesn't my church have this?"

The short answer: somewhere along the way, we traded the unpredictable movement of the Spirit for the predictable safety of programs. We chose control over chaos. Management over miracles. And that drift happened slowly—one half degree at a time until we ended up miles from where we started.

But right now, what matters isn't analyzing what went wrong in the past. What matters is what you're going to do moving forward.

What This Means for YOU

"But you will receive power when the Holy Spirit has come upon you; and you shall be My witnesses both in Jerusalem and in all Judea, and Samaria, and as far as the remotest part of the earth." Acts 1:8 (NASB 1995)

Here's what you need to understand:

Holy Spirit is not locked inside some building.

He's not reserved for Sunday mornings. He's not controlled by pastors or denominations or seminary degrees. He doesn't wait for permission from church boards or approval from elders who've spent decades managing programs instead of pursuing His presence.

Holy Spirit is available to YOU. Directly. Right now.

Jesus didn't say, "You must wait until you know me better before I grant you the baptism of fire." He said, "You will receive power when the Holy Spirit comes upon you."

Not might. Not maybe. Not if your church leadership approves it.

You WILL receive power.
And that power wasn't meant to sit dormant while you wait for someone else to give you permission to use it. It was meant to explode out of you—into your home, your family, your workplace, your neighborhood, everywhere you go.

You don't need a title to walk in Holy Spirit power.

You don't need a seminary degree to hear God's voice.

You don't need to be ordained to pray for the sick, cast out demons, or make disciples.

You don't need a platform to carry fire.

What you need is to surrender. And hunger. And a willingness to pursue God even when the building you're sitting in doesn't. So, what does that look like practically?

Stop waiting.
Stop waiting for your pastor to preach about spiritual gifts.
Stop waiting for your church to make room for Holy Spirit

to move. Stop waiting for someone to give you permission to step into what Jesus already said is yours.

Seek Him yourself.
Pray. Read the Word. Tell Holy Spirit you want His fire. Find people who ARE walking in power as mentors, friends, or other believers who carry what you're hungry for and learn from them.

Don't mistake polish for presence.

Loud music isn't Holy Spirit. A well-structured sermon isn't the same as a rhema word from God. A full building doesn't mean the Spirit is moving. Learn to discern the difference between performance and power.

And that means you become what you're looking for.

If you're hungry for real discipleship? Start discipling with someone. If you want to see the gifts of the Spirit in operation, ask God to use you. If you're tired of dead religion? Become living proof that Jesus is still alive and still moving.

The Church isn't something you find. It's something you ARE.

And it starts the moment you stop waiting for the building to give you what Jesus already promised you could have.

How to Recognize the Real Thing

So how do you know when you've found it? How do you recognize a church, a community, or even a single person who's carrying the real thing?

"You will know them by their fruits. Grapes are not gathered from thorn bushes, nor figs from thistles, are they?" Matthew 7:16 (LSB)

Because here's the problem: counterfeits look good. They sound spiritual. They use all the right words. They might even quote more Scripture than the ones who actually walk in power. But Jesus gave us a simple test: Look at the fruit.

Not the budget. Not the attendance numbers. Not the production quality or the social media following. *The fruit.*

Here's what to look for:
Are people actually being transformed? Not just "inspired" for a weekend. Not just emotionally moved by a worship set. But it genuinely changed. Delivered from addiction and healed from trauma. Set free from sin patterns that held them for years—walking and living in Holy Spirit, prophesying or speaking in tongues, and operating in their spiritual gifts.
Suppose all you see is the same people sitting in the same seats year after year with the same struggles; that's not transformation. That's religious attendance.

You can believe in Jesus, be baptized in water, and not be baptized in the Spirit. Not because He isn't available, but because you didn't "receive" Him. This book is the result of this exact experience. I was saved and called to preach at the age of 9. I didn't meet or even hear about Holy Spirit until He came and found me and brought me to Him in a church in Colorado Springs. Nearly ten years had passed before I received Him into my life. Not just any Church, but one I could grow in and learn who I was in the kingdom.

How can you receive something you've never experienced or ever heard of?

Are disciples being made, or just attendees being managed?

Jesus said, "Go and make disciples." Not "go and fill seats." A disciple isn't someone who shows up on Sunday. A disciple is someone who's learning to walk like Jesus, talk like Jesus, love like Jesus, and carry the power Jesus promised.

If the Church is focused on growth strategies instead of discipleship, you're looking at a business, not the body of Christ.

Is there room for Holy Spirit to move, or just room for the schedule? When's the last time you saw a service go off script because the Spirit was moving?

When's the last time someone prophesied? When's the last time the sick were prayed over and actually healed? When's the last time the music stopped because someone needed prayer, and the whole church laid hands on them?

If everything is predictable, polished, and runs exactly on time every week, you might be watching a performance, not experiencing God's presence.

If you look at the back wall display and it has a timer on it, chances are it's a performance not designed to let the Spirit show up to interrupt the schedule.

Are the leaders walking in what they're preaching? Do they catch fire, or just talk about it? Do they move in spiritual gifts, or just teach them in the past tense? Does Holy Spirit lead them, or are they system-dependent? Do they hear from God, or just prepare sermons?

You can't follow someone into a place they've never been.

Is there hunger for MORE, or satisfaction with "good enough"?

A Spirit-filled community is never satisfied. They're always pressing in and always seeking. Always hungry for more of God. They don't coast. They don't plateau. They don't settle for "we've always done it this way."

If the leadership seems content with the status quo, you're not in a place that's chasing after God's heart.

Here's the bottom line:
Don't be impressed by buildings, budgets, or brands. Don't be fooled by lights, fog machines, or professional production. Don't mistake theological correctness for spiritual power. Don't be taken in by host teams and areas

of service, but no prayer and laying on of hands or anointing with oil.

Look for fruit. Look for fire. Look for the undeniable presence of God that changes lives.

And if you can't find it in the building you're sitting in?

Then maybe it's time to stop looking for a building and start becoming the Church yourself.

You ARE the Ekklesia

"But you are a chosen race, a royal priesthood, a holy nation, a people for God's own possession, so that you may proclaim the excellencies of Him who has called you out of darkness into His marvelous light." 1 Peter 2:9

So, here's where we land. Whether your church gets it or not, whether your pastor walks in fire or manages programs, whether the building you sit in is full of Holy Spirit or full of smoke machines . . . *You are still called.*

You are still chosen. You are still part of the body of believers—the called-out ones. Not because of where you attend, but because of who lives in you.

The Church isn't a place. It's a people. And if Holy Spirit is in you, then YOU are part of it. Right now. Today. In your home, in your workplace, in your neighborhood.

The generation rising up doesn't need another polished service. They need to see Jesus alive in YOU. They need to see someone who actually walks in the power they read about in Acts. Someone who hears from God. Someone who prays and things happen. Someone who isn't afraid to lay hands on the sick, speak truth in love, and live surrendered to Holy Spirit instead of the system.

You don't need permission from some church. You just need obedience.

You don't need a platform or a stage. You only need a personal relationship with the Holy Spirit, who's been waiting for you to stop looking for Him in buildings and start recognizing Him in yourself.

Start where you are.

If you're a parent, disciple your children, prophecy over them, declare them to be children of God, and protected inside the kingdom. Let them see you pray with power, not just routine. Let them see you move when the Spirit moves, not just when it's convenient.

If you're a spouse, be the spiritual leader or support in your home. Pray together. Seek God together. Let your marriage be a picture of what it looks like when two people walk in fire. Declare your marriage holy and sanctified before God! Pray for each other together and apart.

If you're single, find other hungry believers. Meet in homes. Break bread. Bake bread. Eat a meal together every week. Pray for each other. Carry each other's burdens. Be the Ekklesia the way Acts 2 described it as daily, intimate, walking in step with the Spirit.

If you're young, don't wait for permission from older generations who've settled. Pursue God and His Holy Spirit with everything you have. Let your hunger provoke those around you.

Don't be like me and think that you have time because someone told you to wait. IF God called you today, it's because HE has something for you to do today!

The fire has to start somewhere. Why not with you?

The bride of Christ isn't sleeping in a building. She's waking up in living rooms, garages, coffee shops, and anywhere people decide they're done with performance and ready for His presence. They're tired of knowing there's something inside of them that's missing or void. They begin to understand it's a place where our spirit resides. If we don't fill it with Jesus, the devil will fill it with hate.

This is your invitation. Not to find the perfect church. But to BE the Ekklesia Jesus intended. You may be the spark that church down the street needs. Or the home where others can come to find a spark for themselves.

Will you accept it?

"For where two or three have gathered together in My name, I am there in their midst." Matthew 18:20 (LSB)

Jesus tells us in *John 14:14, "If you ask Me anything in My name, I will do it."* That statement comes with so much power that when you are gathered together and ask for something, and it doesn't exist, it will be created for the glory of the kingdom.

That word *"anything"* doesn't mean selfish demands or wishful thinking.

It means *alignment* with the heart of the Father. It means when your life is surrendered, and your spirit is in step with His, you can speak things into being. Not because you're powerful, but because *He is* and *He promised.*

And yes—when two or more are gathered in His name, there is power to pull from heaven what doesn't even exist on earth yet.

Not to impress.
Not to entertain.
But to bring glory to the Kingdom.
Salvation to a people.
Healing the sick and dying.

You're not asking God to do magic.
You're asking the King to *back His Word . . . and* He always does.

Chapter 21

Discovering Your Calling

Why We Resist the Fire

"for the gifts and the calling of God are irrevocable." Romans 11:29 (LSB)

What if the power you've been avoiding is the very thing that awakens your calling? Holy Spirit doesn't fit into schedules, denominations, or comfort zones. He doesn't fit into a class or profession. He doesn't come to entertain, He comes to ignite, to guide, and to light the way. But before He commissions, He confronts.

"But when He comes, He will convict the world regarding sin, and righteousness, and judgment." John 16:8

The fire of the Spirit is uncomfortable, unpredictable, untamable, and uncontrollable. We've stood by and watched the Westernized Church train preachers, not pastors—Evangelists and teachers, but not prophets.

Seminaries taught theology but not relationship, the knowledge of God but not the mechanics of leading the flock or administering a church. A division of theology occurred, and suddenly, a cessation of spiritual gifts became doctrine. Then we began preparing worship leaders for safety, not surrender.

But Holy Spirit doesn't follow the doctrines and beliefs of man. Denominations and traditions do not control Him. Not reduced by how uncomfortable we are. God's Spirit will not be silenced.

"These people honor Me with their lips, but their heart is far from Me. And in vain do they worship Me, teaching as doctrines the commandments of men."
Matthew 15:8–9 (LSB)

At The Root of The Tree

Seminaries mainly taught theology, but not much about relationships. They trained men to study the Bible, not walk with people. They taught how to preach, but not how to listen. They never covered how to lead a body, handle conflict, or carry a church through grief.

They didn't teach how to pray with the broken, how to deal with burnout, or how to follow Holy Spirit when the plan falls apart.

Over time, the classroom replaced the altar. We value knowledge more than intimacy. We valued instruction over discipleship. We valued structure more than surrender, and order more than the move of God within us.

Then came a theological divide, a slow drift, a cold doctrine. Cessationism crept in, and suddenly, those spiritual gifts were labeled fanaticism.

We stopped making room for power and began making excuses as to why it didn't show up.

The Lie That the Fire Was Only for the First Twelve

Nowhere in Scripture does it say that only the twelve apostles would do greater works than Jesus. That belief isn't just a misunderstanding; it is rebellion dressed up like reverence. It's a Pharisee spirit with a seminary degree. All the knowledge, none of the fire.

It takes a certain kind of blindness to read about the gifts of the Spirit, the fire at Pentecost, the miracles in Acts, and then say, "That was only for them."

First off, it lacks common sense. Second, it breaks with Scripture. And third, it always seems to come from the ones who are most afraid of losing control.

"Truly, truly I say to you, the one who believes in me, the works that I do, he will do also; and greater works than these he will do, because I am going to the Father."
John 14:12 (LSB)

That verse has no expiration date. No footnote saying, "This applies to Peter, James, and John only." It says, *"the one who believes in Me."* That's you and me. That's right here and right now!

Why the Gifts Haven't Stopped—But We Did

Cessationism is a doctrine born out of fear, not faith. A theology of control. It gives people a reason to ignore what they can't explain. To reject the fire, they can't contain it.

"God also testifying with them, both by signs and wonders, and by various miracles and by gifts of the Holy Spirit according to His own will." Hebrews 2:4

If God is the same yesterday, today, and tomorrow:

"Jesus Christ is the same yesterday and today, and forever." Hebrews 13:8 (LSB)

If the gifts were only for the first century, then why would Paul teach the Corinthians how to use them so well, and not how to bury them? If the fire ended after Acts, then why would Jesus say the Spirit would be with us *forever*?

"And I will ask the Father, and He will give you another Helper, so that He may be with you forever."
John 14:16 (LSB)

Forever didn't just mean forty years back then, and it isn't ending now!

Mankind asks for and often demands order. Holy Spirit brings interruption.

Humans want to know what's next; they want control. Jesus demands we pick up our cross to follow Him and surrender. The world and man fear the fire, but it's the fire that removes the dross and purifies.

Repentance, Not Judgment

This isn't an attack on the Church, nor is it an argument of theology. It's a wake-up call to the one Church, not the geo-location of a place of worship, but the geo-location of man's heart. His soul and the Spirit inside it.

It is in these moments that truth gets defined by God, not tradition. The moment faith and discernment overpower habits. When surrender matters more than filled seats. When repentance matters more than reputation.

We don't need more attendance and tithes for our programs. We need a continuous presence of Holy Spirit. We don't need more polish on social media and big screen TVs. We need the power of God to be passed through the hands of pastors and elders to heal the sick, make the deaf hear, and the blind see.

What we need are surrendered saints, humble, holy, and willing to serve at all costs.

The silence of our compromise from the pulpit has created weakness in our spirits, in our marriages, and in our homes. It has cast a shadow over the ordained roles God gave to the spiritual head of our homes. The enemy has turned what was sacred into a part-time commitment instead of a covenant before God and before man.

"These signs will accompany those who have believed: in My name they will cast out demons, they will speak with new tongues, they will pick up serpents, and if they drink any deadly poison, it will not harm them; they will lay hands on the sick, and they will recover."
Mark 16:17–18 (NASB 1995)

This wasn't reserved for the apostles. It was a sign for every believer then and now. Jesus didn't say these signs *might* follow the Church. He said they *will.* And they aren't for stage shows or spiritual elites. They're for the faithful. For the surrendered.

"On that day the deaf will hear words of a book, and out of their gloom and darkness the eyes of those who are blind will see. The afflicted also will increase their joy in the Lord, and the needy of mankind will rejoice in the Holy One of Israel." Isaiah 29:18–19 (LSB)

The power Jesus promised in Mark is the same awakening Isaiah prophesied. Healing. Joy. Eyes opened. Voices lifted. Not just for *the first believers* in Acts, but for *this generation*. For the believers who are ready to say yes to fire.

In Greek, it's not a suggestion. It's not *those who sort of believed for a moment*. It's *"those who have believed"—decisively, fully, permanently.*

The kind of belief that puts your feet in the fire and your hands on the sick.

What Move of the Spirit Have You Feared?

When I was young, sitting in a Baptist church in Oklahoma, we were all told that tongues are not something we do, not something we believe in. I stood with a bowed head through many invitations, waiting and watching for someone to be saved. Silence.

Not one person was invited to come and be anointed with oil and prayed over for God to heal them of their cancer, their heart disease, or any other ailment. If we got sick, I was never told to pray, just to take this medicine and rest. I guess we didn't believe in that either.

"Is anyone among you sick? Then he must call for the elders of the church, and they are to pray over him, anointing him with oil in the name of the Lord; and the prayer of faith will restore the one who is sick, and the Lord will raise him up, and if he has committed sins, they will be forgiven him." James 5:14–15 (LSB)

Where many of us get lost in this verse is at the very end. It would be clearer if we understood that forgiveness comes first. If we aren't in alignment with the Father, if we haven't repented of our sins and forgiven others for theirs, then how can we be restored?

Why would we be restored if we weren't walking in love toward God and others in that moment?

"Therefore, if you are presenting your offering at the altar, and there you remember that your brother has something against you, leave your offering there before the altar and go; first be reconciled to your brother, and then come and present your offering." Matthew 5:23–24 (LSB)

We say we want healing. But God wants alignment. He's not a vending machine for miracles. He's a Holy Father looking for sons who walk clean.

You can't hold bitterness in one hand and ask for a blessing with the other.

You can't curse your brother and expect healing from the same mouth.

Before you ask to be healed, ask whether you've repented of your sin and forgiven those who have sinned against you. Ask Holy Spirit whether you're right with Him, whether He abides in you and you in Him because the fire doesn't fall on performance. It falls on surrender.

What calling have you delayed because it didn't feel "safe"?

"It was by faith that Abraham obeyed when God called him to leave home and go to another land that God would give him as his inheritance. He went without knowing where he was going." Hebrews 11:8 (NLT)

Your Calling Isn't an Accident

God didn't put that fire in you just to let it sit still. He didn't fill you with His Spirit so you could play it safe. You don't wait to step into your calling once you've got it all figured out. You step into it when you finally say yes.

Maybe you've been waiting on permission, on clarity, on a sign you can't ignore. Don't wait. Pray yes, but don't try to tell God what you can and cannot do.

What if the fire you're feeling right now is the sign?

You don't need a program or a diploma. You don't need a title. You need to surrender. Sometimes the next step is the one that makes your knees shake. That's where the Spirit tends to lead.

The Church doesn't need more devout and knowledgeable people sitting in pews, waiting to feel qualified. To be released into their purpose.

It needs surrendered ones who know they aren't quite there yet, but show up anyway because they know who is with them.

"Now to Him who is able to do far more abundantly beyond all that we ask or think, according to the power that works within us." Ephesians 3:20 (LSB)

That power that is in Jesus is in you. Not someday. Not once you've earned it. Right now. Your greatest friend is Holy Spirit if you let Him be that for you.

So, what's your next step?

Are you going to stop waiting for it to be easy?

Stop waiting for God's calling to feel safe?

Take that first step and start walking toward that *one thing* God won't let you forget. That heart-shaking nudge that keeps leaning in. Be patient; it may end up being 40 years later before a part of that journey is fulfilled or comes to an end.

That lingering thought, or often reminder, that comes when you least expect it. That's usually the path God prepared you for and now lights the way.

Chapter 22

Speaking Truth in Love

When Love Refuses to Speak

The Cost of Silence

You watch as someone you know is heading towards a cliff in their marriage. They're not running on purpose. But the direction is constant, and they keep taking the same steps, one after another. They don't see the edge is coming, but you do. You think about shouting just once. Maybe they'll hear. And then you stop.

Maybe it's not your place. Just maybe another friend, someone closer, will warn him. Or . . . maybe he'll figure it out on his own. And so, you stay quiet.

That moment, whether imagined or real, is happening in our churches, families, and friendships every single day. We see sin, self-destruction, and spiritual drift. And instead of speaking, we smile. We tell ourselves it's grace, patience, or kindness. But if love refuses to speak, is it really love? We hope that when we ask how they're doing, their reply is what we've come to expect. That safe, I don't have to pray for them, answer. "I'm alright." "I'm good, and you?"

The modern Church has confused "being nice" with "being loving." We've traded honesty for harmony. But love without truth is just flattery. Truth without love is brutality. Both leave us broken.

I've stood by and not opened my mouth before. I've also spoken up with a sharp tongue and made it worse. Both left a mess. Both taught me something I needed to learn. Silence can bring lifelong regrets. There is always forgiveness if you speak harshly or in anger.

Ephesians 4:15 says it plainly: *"But speaking the truth in love, we are to grow up in all aspects into Him who is the head, that is, Christ."*

Truth and love grow us. Together, they keep us in alignment with the Father. Not one without the other.

The Difference Between Judgment and Discernment

You're Not Called to Judge Hearts, But You Are Called to Guard the Flock

You've heard it before. "Judge not, lest you be judged." It's usually said by someone who doesn't want to be told they're headed off a cliff. Why do you think the Church has gotten quiet? Not because we don't see what's going on, but because we've been told to stay in our lane, keep our mouths shut, and just love people.

But somewhere along the way, we confused loving someone enough to say something with being afraid to offend them. We forgot that love warns. Love protects.

Love pays attention and is ever watchful. And sometimes love calls something sin because it is.

Jesus said not to judge in Matthew 7:1, but He was warning against hypocrisy, not discernment. It's one thing to pretend you're perfect and point fingers. It's another thing entirely to love someone enough to say, "Brother, this is killing you."

Paul didn't stutter in 1 Corinthians 5:12: *"What business is it of mine to judge those outside the church? Are you not to judge those inside?"*

We're not called to condemn the world. But we are called to guard the body. That means we don't ignore sin when it walks into our home group or our men's breakfast, and especially into our marriage.

We deal with it. Not with shame or condemnation, but with truth. Not to win an argument, not to be "right" but to win a brother back.

"Now if your brother sins, go and show him his fault in private; if he listens to you, you have gained your brother. But if he does not listen to you, take one or two more with you, so that on the testimony of two or three witnesses every matter may be confirmed. And if he refuses to listen to them, tell it to the church; and if he refuses to listen even to the church, he is to be to you as a Gentile and a tax collector." Matthew 18:15–17 (NASB 1995)

Matthew 18 lays it out this way: Go to him alone. Then with a witness. Then with the Church. So, the question is:

Are you confronting to restore, or to be right? This isn't about pointing fingers. It's about protecting the ones you've been given to love. That's called obedience.

"Brothers and sisters, even if a person is caught in any wrongdoing, you who are spiritual are to restore such a person in a spirit of gentleness; each one looking to yourself, so that you are not tempted as well."
Galatians 6:1 (LSB)

Galatians 6:1 says to do it gently.

I think at some point growing up, dealing with relationships, we've all had a situation like this. Feelings get hurt, pride gets hurt, and anger even. But did we avert a tragedy, save a friend? Were they forgiving and thankful for standing up to protect them?

Some confrontations will deepen the relationship. Others will end it. There is always a risk. But Matthew 18:17 is clear: if they refuse to listen even to the Church, 'let him be to you as a Gentile and a tax collector.' Some people can't see that you're trying to save them. And when someone refuses correction and drags you down with them, you may have to let them go. That's not judgment, that's protection.

We've all watched someone get destroyed by a relationship they refuse to leave. Sometimes protecting your brother means telling him, 'That person is toxic. You need to walk away.

Guarding the flock doesn't mean you're better than anyone. It means you love them too much to stay silent.

How to Confront Without Crushing

Before you open your mouth, check your heart.

Are you angry?
Are you trying to prove you're right?
Are you genuinely grieved for your brother?

Because if you're coming in hot, fueled by frustration or pride, you're not there to restore, you're there to win. Is this love, or the flesh in a borrowed pulpit?

"Faithful are the wounds of a friend, but deceitful are the kisses of an enemy." Proverbs 27:6 (LSB)

A real friend will wound you if it means saving your life, but will help you put on the bandage. A fake one will watch you bleed out and call it kindness.

Confrontation isn't always an attack. Many times, it's a rescue. But most of us don't have a clue how to do it. We find ourselves tiptoeing around it, and nothing changes… or we drop a hammer and shatter all the glass.

So how do you speak truth without destroying someone? You follow the path Jesus laid out.

First, you pray. Don't just say, "God, fix them, please." Instead, ask, "Is this even mine to carry?" Sometimes God will have you pray instead of speak. And if He does send you, ask for His words. Yours won't come with healing power like His will.

Secondly, keep it amongst yourselves. Don't be a gossip or share without permission. Matthew 18 starts here. Not in a group text. Not at Bible study, but face-to-face and alone. If you're talking about someone instead of to them, you're not helping . . . you're sinning.

Be specific, don't beat around the bush with statements like, "Brother, I'm concerned," or "You're drifting." These are vague and leave room for deflection and misunderstanding. You've got to face it head-on. For instance, "You're treating your wife like an enemy." "You're using again." Call it for what it is.

Here's what Scripture taught me: repentance isn't just for what we did, it's for what we didn't do. The sins of omission. The times we held our tongue when we should have spoken. So, if God is asking you to confront, don't bury it. That silence might be the sin you answer for later.

Learn to listen without needing to respond immediately. You might not know the whole story. Never assume you understand. Listening to understand is very hard for some when you see a solution and want to share. It is better to ask questions first and be clear.

Give them the space and the time to get it out. If they go quiet, don't panic. Silence isn't always resistance; sometimes it's processing. Let them talk or speak in their own time and at their own pace.

Always point to Jesus. The goal isn't guilt, but grace. "Jesus already paid for this. Let's walk through this with Him."

If you love someone, you'll risk the discomfort of confrontation. Because silence isn't always grace, it can be cowardice wearing a religious mask.

When to Walk Away

Not Everyone Will Receive Correction

Some people simply won't listen. No matter how gently you say it. No matter how many times you pray.

This doesn't mean stop praying for them or giving up on them. It does mean separating yourself from a harmful situation or relationship. At times, you must trust Jesus' blood as the answer and not sacrifice your own peace.

"Do not give what is holy to dogs, and do not throw your pearls before swine, lest they trample them under their feet, and turn and tear you to pieces." Matthew 7:6 (LSB)

This isn't name-calling or judgment. This is a warning. Some hearts aren't soft. Some ears aren't open. Some eyes can't see. And when you try to bring correction to someone who's not ready, they'll twist it or turn it on you.

"He who reproves a scoffer gets dishonor for himself, And he who reproves a wicked man gets insults for himself. Do not reprove a scoffer, lest he hate you, Reprove a wise man and he will love you." Proverbs 9:7–8 (NASB 1995)

Before you walk away, ask yourself these questions:

- Have I gone to them more than once?
- Have I followed scripture and brought others with me (Matthew 18)?
- Have I done this with a broken heart and not a bitter one?
- Have I prayed, really prayed?
- What did I hear?
- And am I walking away with a hard heart, or a broken one?

The truth is that some people will choose sin over a relationship. It's a choice we all face at some point in our lives. You can't force someone to repent. You can lead a horse to water, but you can't make him drink.

Jesus said the same thing in different words:

"And whoever does not receive you, nor heed your words, as you leave that house or that city, shake off the dust of your feet." Matthew 10:14 (NASB 1995)

At some point, you hand them to God, shake the dust off, and move on.

Chapter 23

When Men Stay Silent, Everyone Suffers

The Failure to Confront Is a Failure to Love

Men are called to protect. Not just physically, but spiritually. And sometimes protecting someone means protecting them from themselves. But we've gotten so tired and afraid of being "that guy," the judgmental one, the harsh one, that we've stopped protecting anyone at all.

Eli Knew—And Did Nothing

Eli was a priest, a father, and a leader. He knew his sons were corrupt. Sleeping with women at the temple entrance. Stealing sacrifices meant for God and abusing their authority for personal gain. Eli saw it all. And he said something, once. Weakly. Then he let it go.

God didn't just judge Eli's sons. He judged Eli for his silence.

"Why do you honor your sons more than Me?"
1 Samuel 2:29 (LSB)

That question still echoes to this day. You ever stand where Eli stood, watching and doing nothing? Eli's failure to confront didn't keep the peace. It unleashed judgment, and his sons died. His lineage, his legacy, was cut off. All because a father chose comfort over confrontation.

The Modern Problem

We've stood by in the West and watched the enemy build a culture where saying, "You're wrong" gets you labeled as divisive.

It's not just fear of being wrong, it's fear of being rejected. Called judgmental. Harsh. Unloving. So, we stay quiet and call it grace.
We traded truth for tolerance.

And the result? Men stay in sin. Marriages crack open. Kids grow up without fathers willing to speak not just the hard truth, but little truth at all. The Church grew weak, not because the world is too strong, but because we're too afraid to deal with what's rotting us from the inside.

"As for those who persist in sin, rebuke them in the presence of all, so that the rest may stand in fear." 1 Timothy 5:20 (ESV)

The Watchman Warning

God called Ezekiel a watchman. His job? See the sword coming and blow the trumpet. Warn the people. And God said this:

"But if the watchman sees the sword coming and does not blow the trumpet, and the people are not warned, and a sword comes and takes a person from them, he is taken away for his wrongdoing; but I will require his blood from the watchman's hand." Ezekiel 33:6 (LSB)

"If you see it and say nothing, their blood is on you."

So, here's the question you can't dodge:

Who are you refusing to confront because it's uncomfortable?

And what's it going to cost if you don't speak?

Restoration Is the Goal, Not Punishment

We're Not Called to Be the Judge, Jury, and Executioner

Confrontation without restoration is just condemnation dressed up as righteousness. The goal isn't to make someone feel like garbage; it's to bring them back.

But here's the thing: Not everything that looks broken is sin. Sometimes it's grief.

What if they're mad at God?

Imagine a friend losing their oldest son because someone lost their cool and knocked him down, and he never woke up. Don't be afraid to just be present in silence. Don't let yourself feel awkward, like you need to say something.

God is a big God. Don't think He doesn't understand exactly what it's like to lose a son. He does. Don't try to explain their initial anger or need for answers away. God will help with that later.

Now, if it *is* sin you're dealing with, the goal still isn't punishment. It's restoration.

We find this story in John 8, where the Pharisees dragged a woman caught in adultery into the middle of a crowd, right at Jesus' feet. They wanted justice. They wanted blood. But Jesus didn't give them what they wanted.

He bent down and wrote in the dirt. Then He stood and said:

"The one who is without sin among you, let him be the first to throw a stone at her." John 8:7 (LSB)

One by one, they dropped the rocks. And when it was just Jesus and the woman, He said:
"I do not condemn you, either. Go. From now on, do not sin any longer." John 8:11 (LSB)

Jesus didn't excuse her sin. He named it. Then He gave her a way forward. Can you see the difference?

So, what does restoration actually look like in action?

Repentance: Not just "I'm sorry," but a broken heart that turns around—a person who owns their sin and walks away from it, with Jesus.

Accountability: Don't just confront and ghost. Walk with them. Pray *with* them, not just *about* them. Invite God to sit in the mess with you both …He's not afraid of it.

Grace: Remember what I said earlier: *"To give like before."* Give grace the way God does—giving to us like before it ever happened. If God has covered it, don't keep digging it up. Don't become their accuser. Don't make them wear their sin like a name tag.

Community: Don't step back, draw them closer. Bring them back in. Don't freeze them in the worst version of themselves. Let them grow. Offer the grace of forgiveness so they can forgive themselves.

"Brothers and sisters, even if a person is caught in any wrongdoing, you who are spiritual are to restore such a person in a spirit of gentleness; each one looking to yourself, so that you are not tempted as well."
Galatians 6:1 (LSB)

Because tomorrow?

It might be you who needs to be restored.

There was a time in my life when I needed to be restored. Recently divorced, broken in many regards, and self-marked as a failure. I volunteered to go to war for two reasons. One, I thought I could go and maybe save the lives of those who would be under me. Two, I didn't plan on coming home. Selfish, I know. But I had adopted the stereotypical reason of having nothing left to live for.

I wrote a letter, I got one back, and as I've mentioned before, it came with a Bible. His Bible had his notes, his underlined scriptures, but most of all his love that came with it. No judgment, no forgiveness needed, but I knew without a doubt he was praying.

It wasn't his actions or the Bible that restored me, but it was his prayers that were answered, which did just that. I felt like a son again instead of a failure. I met a Father who understood me, and I finally let Him in.

Love Speaks

Silence Isn't Safety

The Church doesn't need more "nice guys." It needs men who love enough to speak the hard truth. Jesus didn't stay silent when people were wrong. He called out hypocrisy. He rebuked Peter. He flipped tables when the house of prayer turned into a market. But He didn't do any of it to prove a point. He did it because He loved them.

If you love someone in the way God loves us, you'll risk the relationship you have with them to save their soul.

The final challenge:

Is there someone God is asking you to confront right now?
Is there a conversation you've been avoiding because it might be uncomfortable?
What is it going to cost if you keep your mouth shut? For them? For you?

"My brothers, if any among you strays from the truth and one turns him back, let him know that he who turns a sinner from the error of his way will save his soul from death and will cover a multitude of sins."
James 5:19–20 (NASB 1995)

Prayer

Father, give me the strength and courage to speak when You ask me to. Give me a love that refuses to let my brothers walk toward chaos and destruction. Give me wisdom to know how and when to speak. To speak in humbleness and gentleness for the encouragement of others. Lord, when I do speak, let it be Your words, not my own. Help me to restore, to rebuild, and not destroy. In Jesus' Holy name, Amen.

Chapter 24

Using Your Gifts in Community

Passing the Flame

You Weren't Saved to Sit

"As each one has received a special gift, employ it in serving one another as good stewards of the multifaceted grace of God." 1 Peter 4:10 (NASB 1995)

You weren't saved just to make it out alive. You weren't rescued from the fire so you could sit on the porch and watch the world burn. You were saved to serve. Not someday. Not when you feel qualified, but now, in this moment and in this place.

God hasn't pulled you out of the darkness of this world so that you could warm a seat or hide in some Bible study group. He gave you something holy to be used, not for decoration to be put on a shelf. Not to boost your good name, but to share His Son's good name, the name of Jesus. A gift given for use in the body, in His mission, for the Kingdom.

Some men try to wear their calling like a badge. Some hide it. Some build platforms instead of altars. But here's the truth: the abilities God gave you to draw people to Him will end up building walls if you use them for yourself.

Serving others is more than thinking about it or believing it's important. Serving is a way of life. It's not a verse to quote. It's having a towel in your hand.

When Jesus, *the Son of God*, got down and washed the dirty feet of His disciples, He wasn't just doing a kind thing. He was showing us the Kingdom in action. No one in the room expected anything like this. And the truth is, most of them probably felt uncomfortable watching it. But He did it anyway.

And then Jesus told them: *"You also ought to wash one another's feet." (John 13:14)* That's the call. To do the small things. The quiet things no one else notices. The things most people think are below their calling or beneath their value. Because the ones who look most like Jesus—*serve like Him.*

"For if anyone thinks he is something when he is nothing, he deceives himself." Galatians 6:3 (LSB)

So, the question isn't *if* you have a gift. You do.

The question is:
What are you doing with it?

Using Your Gift in Community

Have you ever been the "new guy" at work? Guess what, people treat new believers the same way. Scripture does speak of being childlike and growing into maturity. At the beginning of our walk is the time to be obedient and observant. A time to ask questions and gain clarity.

"Therefore, rid yourselves of all malice and all deceit and hypocrisy and envy and all slander, and like newborn babies, long for the pure milk of the word, so that by it you may grow in respect to salvation, if you have tasted the kindness of the Lord."
1 Peter 2:1–3 (NASB 1995)

Walking out that path God set before us is rewarding and life-changing in more ways than one. I've seen those who are on fire and ready to go at a moment's notice. I've watched as others who are on fire go, "Wait, am I ready yet?" We all start somewhere and in our own way. The important part is letting God's Spirit guide us on this walk.

Using your gifts is already showing up in your life. At home, work, when talking with friends and family. What we don't always recognize at first—like being naturally good at something, or seeing things more clearly than others, or having the ability to walk people through celebrations and tragedies—these are all from God, too.

Do you write? Are you good at making videos or photography? How about being a good listener? God knew us before we were born. He knows our strengths and our weaknesses. He designed us to receive our spiritual gifts to help us walk in our calling.

So, for those who thought their mess was going to restrict or limit them, sorry. God's going to use that mess or experience to have you help someone else have a breakthrough or to find Jesus.

When we try to put a name on something like "The gift of writing" or "The gift of speech," we limit what God has in store for us. Titles and labels restrict the power of God. It brings division of purpose within you. Your heart and spirit want to move, but your mind has told you you're better at writing, not speaking.

"All these are empowered by one and the same Spirit, who apportions to each one individually as He wills."
1 Corinthians 12:11 (ESV)

The Gift You Don't Have Isn't the One You Need

Let me be honest with you about something I wrestled with for years.

I wanted to speak in tongues. I had been told by others that if you don't speak in tongues, you haven't been baptized in the Holy Spirit. I heard people say it was the evidence, the proof, the sign you'd received the fire of Holy Spirit like on the day of Pentecost.

Look, I grew up not being taught about any spiritual gifts, and specifically that "we" didn't believe in speaking in tongues. I visited some Pentecostal churches, and it seemed like the whole congregation was speaking in tongues at different times in the service. I thought it might be fake at first glance. No one translated, no one explained anything. But I didn't know.

Then one day, I read a report that 60% of Baptist ministers reported anonymously in a survey that they had a prayer language. Could that be tongues? A prayer language?

So, I prayed for it. I sought it. I felt like I was missing something, like I was spiritually deficient somehow.

And for years, I carried that weight, the sense that I wasn't good enough, that maybe I hadn't surrendered fully, that maybe God was holding something back from me.

But here's what I missed: I was so busy chasing the gift I didn't have that I completely missed the gift I did have.

But because I was fixated on tongues, I almost missed the gift He'd already placed in my hands.

And I doubt seriously if I'm alone in this.

How many people have spent years feeling like second-class believers because they don't speak in tongues, don't teach or prophesy? Or believe that they don't have a gift at all?

How many have doubted their salvation, questioned whether the Spirit really lives in them, or wondered if they're somehow less anointed than the guy next to them who prays in a heavenly language?

Jesus never said, "Believe, and you will receive Holy Spirit and speak in tongues."

Brother, listen to me: that's a lie. And it's a lie that's created division in the body for way too long.

Holy Spirit is not bound by a denomination's statement of faith. He doesn't check the church's doctrinal position before He walks through the door. He goes where He's welcome, and sometimes where He's not, just to prove a point.

The best verse for this:

"The wind blows where it wishes, and you hear its sound, but you do not know where it comes from or where it goes. So it is with everyone who is born of the Spirit." John 3:8 (ESV)

You can't contain Him. You can't policy Him out. You can grieve Him, you can quench Him, but you cannot put walls around where He moves.

The real question underneath your question is this: Can Holy Spirit show up in a church that doesn't believe in tongues without tongues being the evidence that He did? And the answer is yes. Salvation is evidence. Transformation is evidence. A man weeping at an altar who hasn't cried in twenty years is evidence. A marriage restored is evidence. None of that required a prayer language.

Tongues are one gift among many. Holy Spirit is the Giver. The Giver is bigger than any single gift.

Paul asked the Corinthians a direct question:

"All are not apostles, are they? All are not prophets, are they? All are not teachers, are they? All are not workers of miracles, are they? All do not have gifts of healings, do they? All do not speak with tongues, do they? All do not interpret, do they?" 1 Corinthians 12:29-30 (NASB 1995)

The answer to every single one? **No.**

Not everyone has every gift. That's not a bug in God's design; it's the entire point. We're one body. Different parts.

Different functions. All essential. All are empowered by the same Spirit.

"But to each one is given the manifestation of the Spirit for the common good." 1 Corinthians 12:7 (LSB)

No gift on that list outranks another. None. Paul uses the word "greater" in verse 31, but read what he means — not greater in value, greater in usefulness to the room you're standing in. He says it plainly just two chapters later:

"Now I wish that you all spoke in tongues, but rather that you would prophesy; and greater is one who prophesies than one who speaks in tongues, unless he translates, so that the church may receive edifying." 1 Corinthians 14:5 (LSB)

There it is. Greater only means it builds up more people at once. That's it. No hierarchy. No ranking. No first class and coach.

And then Paul drops this:

"And I show you a still more excellent way." 1 Corinthians 12:31 (ESV)

Then comes chapter 13. Love. That's the more excellent way. Not a gift — a way of carrying every gift you have.

God didn't give you the wrong gift. He gave you the right one for the assignment He has for you. Stop measuring yourself against someone else's gift.

Stop feeling deficient.

If Holy Spirit lives in you, you are sealed, filled, and equipped.

Now the question is: are you going to use what God gave you?

How To Steward What God Gave Me

We're going to have to answer some questions here. Where are you? Are you involved with a body of believers already? Are there opportunities to serve?

By serving, I mean anything: mowing the lawn, running a bus ministry, serving at events, making the coffee, showing up to pray, being willing to be prayed for. All of this is ministry. Find where you can serve and step in.

But here's what most of us miss: Serving others is a blessing, and allowing others to bless you is serving. Receive your blessings as well as being the one who serves and blesses others.

What does Jesus tell us about the Church, about Himself, and about the body, His Church having many different members.

There are plenty of sermons and classes that have been taught about the different parts of the body (Church) or its members, whether left and right hands or feet, and all the other functions for the rest of the body.

"Now there are many parts, but one body. And the eye cannot say to the hand, 'I have no need of you'; or again, the head to the feet, 'I have no need of you.' On the contrary, it is much truer that the parts of the body which

seem to be weaker are necessary."
1 Corinthians 12:20–22 (NASB 1995)

We've all been wounded in some way in our lives. Some are less than others. Our experiences in this world have shown us our capacity for anger, hate, love, joy, resilience, fear, strength, and weakness.

Don't expect that because you have a gift, it won't be birthed and refined in the fire the world tries to kill us with. All soldiers in battle suffer. They win, they lose, and they look evil in its face at times. Some get lost, others find truth and life in Jesus.

As Christian soldiers, it is our mission, our assignment, to spread the gospel throughout the world. That part could be anything from preaching at a tent revival in front of ten or in front of thousands. It could be putting up the poles to hold the tent. It could be teaching a child the names of the books of the Bible. Maybe the privilege of teaching the youth or the privilege of cleaning the building after they've gone.

"Just as the Son of Man did not come to be served, but to serve, and to give His life as a ransom for many."
Matthew 20:28 (LSB)

Jesus didn't come to reign the first time. He came to serve. He came to rescue and to love. He came to forgive.

Washing the feet of His disciples was not something they ever expected to see.

How do you become a steward of what God has given? How will you serve?

Don't try to hard to seel your spot; many times, you'll be surprised when someone comes to you.

But always serve.

"If I then, the Lord and the Teacher, washed your feet, you also ought to wash one another's feet. For I gave you an example, so that you also would do just as I did for you." John 13:14–15 (NASB 1995)

What God gives you grows even more when it's given away.

Chapter 25

When God Whispers

Was there a time you felt like you should've said something or done something but decided against it? I remember driving one time, and the name of a friend popped into my head. My first thought was Wow, I haven't thought about him in a while. Then I forgot about it. It wasn't like I could write it down while I was driving. I wouldn't know what to write other than his name.

Later in life, after having an occasion like this to present itself multiple times, I began to wonder something. Maybe I should have prayed for them in that moment. I mean, it wouldn't hurt, right? Maybe I could have called to check on them?

Look, I'm not saying that every time you think of something or someone, you need to stop and pray, or maybe something is wrong. Was that an opportunity to serve? I keep asking God to speak to me. Did He?

"For it is God who is at work in you, both to desire and to work for His good pleasure." Philippians 2:13 (LSB)

A bit of self-reflection in this moment. I've been saying for years, like 15 years, that if "IF" I could write a book, it would be called "Life After John 3:16, What Your Pastor Didn't Tell You." I never saw myself writing this book.

It started with a murmur in 1985 in Mainz, Germany, while serving in the military. I was speaking with a sergeant in my unit about our faith. That was when I told someone for the first time that I felt like God wanted me to write a book. I don't remember telling anyone else. Ever.

What has God been working in me all along?

"For we are His workmanship, created in Christ Jesus for good works, which God prepared beforehand so that we would walk in them." Ephesians 2:10 (LSB)

What has God whispered to you?

And now, years later, here I am. Writing the book God whispered about in 1985. Not because I was ready. Not because I was qualified. But because I finally said yes.

Until this very moment, I hadn't considered the idea that the past forty years might have been my walk in the wilderness?

The Mustard Seed

I don't know what it is about the mustard seed story that keeps coming to me time and time again. Could it be that Jesus is trying to remind me that it only takes a tiny bit of faith to move mountains?

"If you have faith the size of a mustard seed, you will say to this mountain, 'Move from here to there,' and it will move; and nothing will be impossible for you."
Matthew 17:20 (LSB)

I can get a little mischievous at times. I've always looked at my faith in a way in which I view some battles as mountains. The problem is I look past my mountains and envision Pike's Peak or Mount Everest. I think to myself, if I. . . nah, God might get mad at me. But Jesus said it, so do I really have as much faith as a mustard seed? We believe He can move mountains . . . we just quietly wonder if He will for us.

"To each is given the manifestation of the Spirit for the common good." 1 Corinthians 12:7 (ESV)

The common good! I've heard all the excuses why we don't see mountains moving. If it were easy, we'd all be doing it. Will moving Mount Everest to Oklahoma or throwing it into the sea serve the kingdom of God? It would make a bunch of climbers mad for sure. It boils down to how we look at prayer. The power of prayer moves mountains.

"The effective prayer of a righteous man can accomplish much. Elijah was a man with a nature like ours, and he prayed earnestly that it would not rain, and it did not rain on the earth for three years and six months. Then he prayed again, and the sky gave rain, and the earth produced its fruit." James 5:16–18

If we only believe and do not doubt.

Multiplying the Fire

"You then, my child, be strengthened by the grace that is in Christ Jesus, and what you have heard from me in the presence of many witnesses entrust to faithful men, who will be able to teach others also."
2 Timothy 2:1–2 (NASB 1995)

Obedience isn't just serving in the kingdom. It's multiplication. God doesn't just give to help us stand, or to get us through, or to light our way when it's dark. He gave them for us to be able to set others on fire.

Jesus tells the story of a master who gave three servants different amounts to steward while he was gone. Two of them went to work and doubled what they were given. The third buried it out of fear. When the Master came back, he didn't call that humility. He called it wicked and lazy.

That part still stings.

"But his master answered and said to him, 'You wicked, lazy slave, you knew that I reap where I did not sow and gather where I did not scatter seed.'" Matthew 25:26 (LSB)

We don't like that part of the story. We'd rather stay with the encouragement. But the truth is, burying our gift isn't playing it safe. It's disobedience. It's not humility when we refuse to walk in what God gave us. It's fear. And fear, left alone long enough, will bury everything God tried to build in us.

We are the seed planters in the world; the Father is the one who waters them.

What have you buried?

Where have you planted seeds?

What's the Name of Your Fire?

God has placed something inside of you; it's a part of your DNA. You most likely know what it is. Maybe it's teaching. Maybe it's serving. Maybe it's the ability to see people others overlook. Maybe it's encouragement. Maybe it's just showing up when everyone else quits.

Whatever it is, it's not just for you.

It's for the body. It's for the mission. It's for the kingdom.

It's for your purpose.

Here's the question you can't dodge:

What has God given you that you're not using?

And what's it going to cost if you keep it buried?

"For this reason I remind you to kindle afresh the gift of God which is in you through the laying on of my hands. For God has not given us a spirit of timidity, but of power and love and self-discipline." 2 Timothy 1:6–7 (NASB 1995)

Chapter 26

The Ground You're Walking on Is Holy

The question going through my mind is, is my heart genuine? Am I on the right path to knowing God? I don't have to be there yet; I may never fully arrive, but am I on the right path?

"Enter through the narrow gate; for the gate is wide and the way is broad that leads to destruction, and there are many who enter through it. For the gate is narrow and the way is constricted that leads to life, and there are few who find it." Matthew 7:13–14 (LSB)

Which Gate Do I See?

Holy Spirit isn't looking for perfection or knowledge, He's looking for an obedient heart, a complete surrender of things from the world.

"Search me, God, and know my heart; Put me to the test and know my anxious thoughts; And see if there is any hurtful way in me, And lead me in the everlasting way." Psalm 139:23–24 (LSB)

This hunk of clay (our earthly body) that we live in still has some dark corners. Every once in a while, it's a good idea to pray Psalm 139:23-24 out loud and for ourselves. Things that are deeply rooted in us from our experiences and life on this earth can remain hidden.

It doesn't keep you from being on the right path; it is just a path the enemy will use to attack you. Remember their one mission: steal, kill, or destroy. If the world can't fulfill that assignment, they will try to make you ineffective.

So, what path are you really on?

Every fire starts with surrender and a decision.

What Kind of Ground Am I Walking On?

We all have the capacity for the fire of Holy Spirit to burn inside of us. We've all had the seed of the gospel planted within us to grow. What kind of gardener are you? What type of soil are you plowing your furrows in?

Jesus tells us of the different soils that are in this world that the Sower might find. We see this parable relayed in Matthew 13, Mark 4, and Luke 8. It's called the parable of the Sower; however, some might say the parable of the soils.

"Behold, the sower went out to sow; and as he sowed, some seeds fell beside the road, and the birds came and ate them up. Others fell on the rocky places, where they did not have much soil; and they sprang up immediately, because they had no depth of soil. But after the sun rose, they were scorched, and because they had no root, they withered away. Others fell among the thorns, and the thorns came up and choked them out. But others fell on the good soil and yielded a crop, some a hundred, some sixty, and some thirty times as much. The one who has ears, let him hear." Matthew 13:3–9 (LSB)

Then Jesus explains it to His disciples:

"When anyone hears the word of the kingdom and does not understand it, the evil one comes and snatches what has been sown in his heart. This is the one sown with seed beside the road. The one sown with seed on the rocky places, this is the one who hears the word and immediately receives it with joy; yet he has no root in himself, but is only temporary, and when affliction or persecution occurs because of the word, immediately he falls away. And the one sown with seed among the thorns, this is the one who hears the word, and the anxiety of the world and the deceitfulness of wealth choke the word, and it becomes unfruitful. But the one sown with seed on the good soil, this is the one who hears the word and understands it, who indeed bears fruit and produces, some a hundred, some sixty, and some thirty times as much."
Matthew 13:18–23 (LSB)

I am not going to summarize something as important as this parable and its perfect explanation. Jesus speaks for Himself quite well. This story is one we can all relate to. This story is also one of the reasons I began to write this book. I didn't know anyone was out there who would try to steal the seed someone planted in my heart as I began to find Jesus. But there was someone out there doing just that!

Jesus isn't saying you are a certain kind of soil.

Jesus is saying you are a certain kind of surrender.

"If anyone wants to come after Me, he must deny himself, take up his cross daily, and follow Me." Luke 9:23 (LSB)

The soil determines what grows; our choices determine whether the seed survives.

What Does It Cost to Say No?

How many parties have we been invited to that we didn't want to go to? Have you ever missed one and wished you'd gone? We all have a choice to make, and we make it every single day.

"But He said to him, "A man was giving a big dinner, and he invited many. And at the dinner hour, he sent his slave to say to those who had been invited, 'Come, for everything is now ready.'" Luke 14:16–17 (LSB)

The invitations had already gone out. Those who were invited had every opportunity. They had been invited. They had the knowledge. There was a space at the table. But they didn't want to come.

It wasn't that they just didn't show up; they had excuses. Justification. Work. Family. Life. I have a piece of land to go look at. I have a new wife who doesn't like parties.

"And the slave came back and reported this to his master. Then the head of the household became angry and said to his slave, 'Go out at once into the streets and lanes of the city and bring in here the poor and crippled and blind and lame.'" Luke 14:21 (LSB)

God doesn't cancel the feast. He just fills the seats with the hungry. If you don't come, someone else will. If you don't pour out what God has put in you, He'll pass the cup to someone who will. Not because He loves them more, but because the fire has to fall somewhere. And the table will be filled.

If God has been calling, and you've been giving Him "Maybe later," how long until "later" becomes never?

How many times did you feel that nudge, that conviction, the one that pulled on your spirit and pushed it down because you thought you weren't ready or good enough?

That is what this part of the story is for. Not to guilt you. But to warn you: the oil runs out. The fire goes cold. The feast doesn't wait forever.

If the Holy Spirit is speaking now, then now is the time to answer. Not when the stars align. Not when you finally feel "anointed enough." Just now. We make this seem harder than it is. It's simply a decision we have to make daily.

God isn't looking for perfect. He's looking for obedience—a willing heart.

That's the fire that doesn't burn out. But the invitation still stands. And maybe it's already in your hand.
And here's what happens when you finally say yes:
You don't just receive the invitation; you become one who gives it.

Chapter 27

Did You Remember Your Invitation?

Who are you pouring into? Are you already leading someone, even if you don't know it? We touched on this before about someone always watching. If you've got children, they are always watching and listening.

Do you have any friends asking silent questions about faith, or your faith?

How about the people at work or on the job site who notice something different about you, who see your peace? Talk about how real discipleship starts. It begins by being faithful with what you know right now, today, not waiting till you have it all figured out.

Have you had any moments like that lately? Did you experience anything like that at any time in your journey? Thinking back to that moment, do you see or remember who it was and what was said?

Since we are in a moment of reflection, is there anyone, it could be several or maybe just the name of one person, you feel like inviting to get to know Jesus better? Are you called to disciple, teach, serve, or encourage someone else? Is this your time to plant some seeds or rekindle an old fire?

"Let your light shine before others, so that they may see your good works and give glory to your Father who is in heaven." Matthew 5:16 (ESV)

The fire God put in you isn't just to keep you warm. It was meant to light someone else's way. Your obedience might be the answer to a prayer someone else hasn't even prayed yet. God didn't place that gift in you to sit on a shelf. He gave it to be opened and passed on to someone else.

What Am I Really Carrying?

So, who are you walking with?
Who are you pouring into?

Before we talk about who you're walking with, we need to ask: what spirit are you actually carrying?

It's possible to use Jesus' name without walking in His authority. It's possible to do ministry without surrendering. And when that happens, it gets exposed.

"But also some of the Jewish exorcists, who went from place to place, attempted to use the name of the Lord Jesus over those who had evil spirits, saying, 'I order you in the name of Jesus whom Paul preaches!' Now there were seven sons of Sceva, a Jewish chief priest, doing this"
Acts 19:13-14 (LSB)

This statement alone should have stopped them. 'Jesus, whom Paul preaches

They wanted the power without the surrender. There was a wrong heart and definitely wrong thinking here. They didn't care about the man possessed by the demon; they wanted a good story to tell.

"But the evil spirit responded and said to them, 'I recognize Jesus, and I know of Paul, but who are you?' And the man in whom was the evil spirit pounced on them and subdued all of them and overpowered them, so that they fled out of that house naked and wounded."
Acts 19:15-16 (LSB)

When you walk into battle without surrender, don't be surprised if you walk out exposed and defeated. "I know Jesus, and I know of Paul, but who are you?" Can you imagine? Demons aren't the only ones who can spot a fake. People can see it too. They sense it when the heart and intent are wrong, even if the words sound right.

"Some, to be sure, are preaching Christ even from envy and strife, but some also from goodwill; the latter do it out of love, knowing that I am appointed for the defense of the gospel; the former proclaim Christ out of selfish ambition rather than from pure motives, thinking that they are causing me distress in my imprisonment. What then? Only that in every way, whether in pretense or in truth, Christ is proclaimed; and in this I rejoice."
Philippians 1:15–18 (LSB)

That doesn't mean God won't use the words of someone without a heart for God. Jesus spoke of these types of people in Matthew 7:22–23. Paul, as well, mentions that those who preached in the name of Jesus could and would still be used to fulfill God's purpose in someone else's life. We read that in Philippians 1 above.

If counterfeit faith exposes the heart, authentic fellowship restores it.

Who's Walking with Me?

"Do not rebuke a scoffer, or he will hate you; Rebuke a wise person and he will love you. Give instruction to a wise person and he will become still wiser; Teach a righteous person and he will increase his insight."
Proverbs 9:8–9 (LSB)

You weren't meant to carry this fire alone. One of the hardest things we face is simply keeping our fire lit. It takes fuel, and our spirit needs the word and faith to sustain our walk with the Father. I've run out of wood before, run out of road, and I've rinsed and repeated that several times. The battle is real.

When you carry the gift from Holy Spirit, it's like carrying the burden or the cross that comes with it. Our weaknesses become our strengths, or our lowest moments become our greatest victories. We may fight that battle, run out of fuel, and run out of road, but every time we come back, we get closer to victory in Jesus. We get closer to full surrender.

We carry the doubts, too. We're experts at carrying doubt. And we try to do it alone. There were times I told myself, *"This is between me and God."*

That sounded holy. But it was really just me hiding behind the fear of letting go and giving it to God and laying them at the foot of the cross without picking them back up again and again. We're supposed to be able to handle things on our own, right? I don't believe we ever were supposed to have to.

"Therefore, humble yourselves under the mighty hand of God, so that He may exalt you at the proper time, having cast all your anxiety on Him, because He cares about you." 1 Peter 5:6–7 (LSB)

We all have a natural defense mechanism. Some call it our comfort zone. It's easy to explain it that way because when you surrender to God, it's going to let out a scream. "I didn't want what comes with community."

But isolation kills fire. If you try to carry your calling in silence, you will burn out, or worse, you'll burn others.

But iron only sharpens iron when it *rubs against it.* That friction? It feels like friction, but it's called connection. That's what shapes the edge.

"Iron sharpens iron, and one man sharpens another." Proverbs 27:17 (ESV)

It's really easy to show up and slip in unnoticed. It's not so easy when you walk in and you are known by someone there. Known by God.

Easier to sit there and nod during a sermon than to say, *"Brother, I'm struggling. Can you pray with me?"* Or better yet, "Brother, do you need someone to pray for you?"

God designed us to be sharpened. To have an edge. Not just be encouraged or gifted.

Not perfect. Just willing. Just obedient. In love with the Father.

Every step we take together in the kingdom is a step deeper into surrender.

This journey was forged in fire. Not the kind that destroys, but the kind that refines. A season of repentance, reflection, and return.

Like Daniel, I've wrestled through the nights. Like Jacob, I'm crossing over. And like you, I'm learning that every fire worth walking through leads us closer to the voice of God.

The ground you're standing on is holy — not because it's perfect, but because He's standing there with you.

Final Prayer

The Fire That Remains

My Prayer for You:

Father God, thank You for this wonderful and glorious day of completion. For those who sit with You now, reading this prayer, let them never walk again in silence, never again feel alone. If there be a new fire or an old flame rekindled, let it burn bright, hot, and bold—with enough wind to breathe it into those around them.

And if, by chance, there stands another like me, who tried to carry that cross alone, remind them: Jesus' blood was already spilled over that cross—over that burden.

Oh, Holy Spirit, come in this moment—with fire, with words our hearts aren't able to speak for ourselves. Father, for those we meet who greet us with a smile, help us see through to the reality of their need and pray for them in that moment.

Father, for those who don't believe, who are skeptical of Your Word, Your power, and even the miracles You've performed in my life—never forget them. Send a brother, a sister, a friend to help turn their face from the world and toward their Savior, Jesus Christ our Lord.

No more silent nights. No more sitting on the back row.

Now, Father, bring us all to the dinner table with our lamps filled with oil. May our words be gentle and kind, filled with grace, yet also with boldness and courage. Fill us with your great love and understanding— with Your wisdom that keeps us humble. Let our joy be our strength, which comes from you.

Let our lamps never grow dim or burn out in the presence of one another. Bring us to the kingdom of promise; bring us home in You. Father, dwell anew in our hearts and in our spirits while we walk on this earth and let our light shine for others to see.

In the name of Jesus, and by the power of His blood shed for me and with the authority of the Kingdom of God—so let it be this day. Amen.

Are you ready for the next Hallelujah!

Some people will tell you, “Your time will come" or "your time is now!"

It took the Israelites 40 years to reach the Promised Land. It took me 40 years to say yes to this book.

But for you? It could be 40 minutes. Or 40 seconds.

The question isn't when. The question is: will you say yes?

My time began the moment I said yes to Jesus; every other yes or no answer was just a bump in the road to get here.

So, if you're waiting—make sure you're waiting on God. And not the other way around.

Acknowledgments

Scripture Quotations

Scripture quotations are taken from multiple translations to bring clarity and depth to God's Word:

www.ingramcontent.com/pod-product-compliance
Lightning Source LLC
LaVergne TN
LVHW090601110826
845146LV00001B/209